In the Beginning, Exodus:
The Bible Then and Now

Andrew P. Porter

WIPF & STOCK · Eugene, Oregon

IN THE BEGINNING, EXODUS
The Bible Then and Now

ISBN 13: 978-1-55635-310-9

www.wipfandstock.com

Manufactured in the U.S.A.

For an old friend, and all like her

Contents

Acknowledgements

Many people have contributed ideas for this book.

Edward Hobbs's theology appears on nearly every page, and the few citations don't do him justice. The entire argument about exposure, limitation, and need was his long before it was ever mine, and the arguments about Exodus typology in the New Testament likewise. The attentive reader will quickly see that without those two premises, the inquiry here could never have gotten started.

Shaun Sullivan does not appear in the book, but many years ago I read the sociology of the early Peter Berger with him, and inasmuch as Berger's work sits everywhere in the background, Shaun Sullivan stands behind that conceptual inheritance. In a sense, Berger's work in sociology of knowledge provides empirical warrant for H. Richard Niebuhr's commitment to confessionality as a theological method.

What I didn't learn about the "Old" Testament from Edward Hobbs I learned from Donn Morgan. None of Donn, Edward, or Shaun are responsible for anything here, but if credit is to be given, much of it should go to them.

Louise Ridsdale asked shrewd questions without which important parts of the book might never have happened. Huston Smith did as much in other places.

Jerine Watson, Jim Lyle, and Elizabeth Wolfe read entire drafts. I am indebted to them for many comments, not all of which I have heeded.

Dennis Roby, Ed Beutner, Adam Peck, and Jerry Ball contributed in many conversations in ways too numerous to count. Bruce Bramlett reminded me of the importance of Zakhor, a problem which lies mostly outside what this book can deal with. Victor Gold, Edward Hobbs, Barbara Green, OP, and Mike Guinan, OFM, helped with recent OT scholarship.

Lowell Wood and Frederick T. Aldridge, in their unintentional but gallant way, created a world in which some of the ideas in this book might actually make sense.

This book was typeset with LaTeX on a Debian Gnu Linux box.

Introduction

This is a book about the Bible, about how it was put together long ago, and about how modern scholars figured out *how* it was put together long ago. It is also about how we became perplexed in the modern world, how biblical religion came to seem so preposterous to so many. What students learn about the Bible and the modern world is too complicated to tell from the pulpit. Nevertheless, it can be life-changing. It makes the Bible come alive, it makes the Bible really real.

Some of it may be frightening, but should not be. Some say it doesn't matter (it's just history, and history doesn't matter). Some think it esoteric knowledge, best saved for professionals, not something to tell ordinary people.

This book is for people willing to look at history. This book is for people who wonder whether history might be the solution and not the problem. This book is for people who want to hear some good news about religion and the Bible in the modern world. And this book is for pastors who know more than they can tell on a Sunday morning.

There is a lot that is not here; only a few problems in recent theology appear in these short pages, and then only tentatively. I once listened to my pastor talking to an RCIA meeting, and he promised to answer candidly questions from the catechumens and candidates, but said he did not have answers to all questions. I think that is exactly the right attitude. For the foreseeable future, there will still be unsolved problems in theology. We live *in statu viatoris*, as people on a pilgrimage in history that is not yet completed. We are comfortable with that in the sciences, where we also remain ignorant of much of the natural world, and we can live with unanswered questions in science. Yet we are not comfortable with unanswered questions in theology. Living on pilgrimage, living with an unknown and risky future, is much older in biblical religion than it is in the sciences. We can do it again.

Many take the question of "science and religion" to be *the* central issue for theology today. I think science is not the central theological problem today. History is.

What is here is a tour through a few events in the history of biblical religion. It begins before the beginnings, and then does the story of Israelite religion. History matters in a historical religion.

After Israelite religion, we shall see the Disasters of the First Century, out of which came the Church and the Synagogue. For all the carnage on the long road from the ancient to the modern world, things were more stable than they might have seemed, but in recent centuries, the world has come apart and "religion" doesn't make sense any more. There begin our current perplexities: we don't know what to do, we have forgotten how the medieval world worked, and we couldn't get back to it even if we could remember it.

So we shift modes at the end, in order to sort things out. There is nothing like a system here, but a few things can be said. When it is over, the world (and biblical religion in it) will appear differently. Hopefully it will then be possible to recognize a world that should have been familiar all along.

The story of Israelite religion is told in tandem with the older explanation of how the Bible came to be written: "JEDP and all that"—the Documentary Hypothesis. That theory says that the Pentateuch, the first five books of the Bible, passed through the hands of four editors, each known by one of the letters of "JEDP." That theory comes from the middle of the nineteenth century, and it has been taught to seminarians and scholars since then. J and E were early sources, with distinctive narrative styles. We come to them below. D is Deuteronomy, and P is the Priestly editor; they, too, have distinctive styles, and noticeably different interests. It all came together around the time of the Babylonian Exile, from a little before to a little after.

Before the documentary hypothesis was the traditional explanation, more or less supernatural, that God determined the wording, and Moses wrote it down; hence the "five books of Moses." After the documentary hypothesis—well, things are not so clear. The hypothesis still lives, but with much less confidence than it once got. D and P are distinctive enough to survive, but the rest, the "JE" stuff, is miscellaneous. There is no consensus on dating the various parts, nor on how to handle what's not D and not P. What *does* survive from the documentary hypothesis, with great confidence, is that these texts are edited documents, from many sources, many traditions, from a human culture in part historically accessible and in part probably not recoverable. The supernatural explanation is gone for good. That will take us in the end to the question of how ordinary believers relate to the history of biblical religion, a question that marks the end of the present inquiry; it would be too much for this book, and even technical explanations are scarce, though a little can be said here.

The reader will quickly see how dependent I am on secondary sources; I am not a biblical scholar, only a philosophical theologian. So this book can hardly qualify even as a popularization of serious biblical scholarship, though it may help the reader find better introductions than this one. The best way to indicate my debts is simply to say a little about a few of the books that were my guides in the story that follows. Readers who want more excitement would probably do well just to go directly to chapter 1.

The books that follow are presented in a semi-chronological order: that is, from those that tell about aboriginal religion and biblical religion to those that tell about how modern scholars recovered the biblical history. The philosophy and theology to make sense of it come last. Eliade, *Cosmos and History*, and Westphal, *God, Guilt, and Death*, are the most important. Hans Walter Wolff and Walter Brueggemann,

The Vitality of Old Testament Traditions, is somewhat technical, but it is the clearest brief exposition of the theological situations from which the Pentateuch emerged during the Israelite monarchy: the period after David and Solomon. John Courtney Murray, *The Problem of God*, argues that our problem is more like the biblical problem of God than it is either the medieval or modern problems of God: we don't have proofs of God, we have anxieties about living in history, and we should not be afraid of our anxieties.

H. Richard Niebuhr's short essay, "Faith in Gods and in God," reprinted in *Radical Monotheism and Western Culture*, deserves some explanation. It was recommended to me by Edward Hobbs. Things come to a climax on p. 122, when Niebuhr announces that "the causes for which we live all die," and that this condition of life and the world is the product of a God who seems an enemy, but is not. "The strange thing has happened that we have been enabled to say of this reality, of this last power in which we live and move and have our being, 'Though it slay us, yet will we trust it.'" Edward Hobbs put it in more concrete terms by saying that the disappointments of life (exposure, limitation, and need), each bring blessing, much though they may hurt. Briefly, exposure happens when I get caught red-handed, and so offered a chance to change; the limitations of life are the raw material of creativity; and need, other people's need, offers fellowship and an opportunity for community. These three, exposure, limitation, and need, will be a major theme in this book, and what follows is a story of how they play out in the modern world.

They come in degrees of severity, from mere inconvenience, to suffering, to appalling affliction. To embrace life as good in full face of these pains is not easy, nor should I say it is. The pains destroy us in the end. Anyone who wants to get out of biblical religion can easily do so just by saying that the pains of life hurt too much; and if that is not bad enough, he can say that history is bunk, and so a historical religion is absurd. (I think those are the real reasons people reject biblical religion. Complaints about science and religion won't stand up to inspection, but that's a long story, only a little of which gets told below.)

When I first heard the series exposure, limitation, and need, it became clear immediately that science was no longer the principal challenge for theology, nor even is science a problem. If you can find and accept the good that comes in exposure, limitation, and need, then nothing can harm you, though many things can hurt you. All problems in theology become solvable, even if they are not solvable *now*. And we need no longer worry about "miracles" as violations of natural laws.

In the modern world, history, "critical history," finding out that the past is not what we traditionally thought it was, is a species of exposure. Relativity, cultural relativity, in which we are both enabled and constrained by what our culture gives us, is a species of limitation. And religious pluralism, the presence of people from other cultures and religions, is a species of need, the need for fellowship. History, relativity, and pluralism are the real challenges to theology and biblical faith today; not science.

If trust in meeting God in exposure, limitation, and need is a general form of faith, then trust in meeting God in history, relativity, and pluralism is the form of faith working itself out in history and community in the present. The faith we can have today is foreshadowed in the biblical record, the story of a people moving from aboriginal nature religion into historical religion. It was a long process of change, one not entirely finished even today, and it was a journey with much anxiety. They thrilled in that anxiety.

Chapter 1

Bewildered

1.1 More Miraculous Than He Knows

Once upon a summer evening, two of my friends were driving north from UCLA to Yosemite. The circumstances are not entirely clear. Some say it was merely the time of the Watts riots, and very hot. Others say that one of these graduate student miscreants had poured just a wee bit too much liquid nitrogen on the Chemistry Department chairman's pride, and their friends told them to get out of town for a few days, for their own good.

In any case, they had gotten about as far as Bakersfield, when, on the radio, lo and behold, an evangelist began to warm up his crowd. He had a live studio audience as well as all the fans out in radio-land. You heard the typical revival meeting radio patter; prayer shawls, put your hands on the radio, let me pray for you, and so on.

It seems he had seven cripples in various stages of terminal illness up on the stage. Most had crutches or wheelchairs or other visible badges of decrepitude. The evangelist interviewed each one in turn. And each said in effect, "I'm looking at you now, but in a few days, I'll be gone." All were diagnosed as terminal, soon to expire; immediately, if the prayer went on too long.

He asked the audience, will it be a miracle if only one of these seven gets up and walks? A tepid but audible "Yes" from the audience. He worked on them some more, about trust in the Lord, and whatnot. "Lord help these people to see their way to support me in this great work." You know the drill.

"Will it be a miracle if even two of them get up and walk?"

(Louder) "Yes!"

More theology, if you can bear to call it that. More encouragement. And by the way, all you folks out there in radio-land, please put your hands on the radio and pray with us. It will never happen if your heart is not in the Lord!

"Will it be a miracle if three of them get up and walk?"

(A little louder) "Yes!"

An interlude about support for this wonderful ministry (i.e., please send money).

"Will it be a miracle if as many as four of them get up and walk?"

(Louder still) "Yes!"

And so on. By the time he got to asking about a miracle if all seven threw away their crutches and walked, the audience was in a frenzy, wild with anticipation.

And then he went through the series again, and one by one, these cripples each got up and walked. "Number one is getting up; . . . Number two is getting up; . . . Number three is getting up; . . ." and so on. The noise grew in a crescendo, the audience roared its delight at each one.

My friends listened in rapt silence all the while, and then one of them turned to the other and deadpanned, "It's seven-factorial more miraculous than he knows: They stood up in numerical order!"

Factorials are the bread and butter of chemistry students; they use them to compute how probable or improbable a chemical reaction is. Seven factorial is $7 \cdot 6 \cdot 5 \cdot 4 \cdot 3 \cdot 2 \cdot 1$, or 5040, the number of different ways in which seven things can be ordered. The probability of them standing up in order *by chance* is one in 5040, not a large number.

Which leaves the possibility of something other than chance.

Entertaining, perhaps. But how on earth did biblical religion get into this sorry state of degeneration? What the culture knows about it is that it is supposed to work miracles, but the miracles are a fraud? (And modern medicine, by the way, does deliver the miracles.) Supposedly biblical religion of the Christian variety, when it appears as the "real thing," is about miracles, Fundamentalism and biblical literalism. There is no other way to read the Bible. And Liberal Theology, when you find it, is just the same thing diluted, like chicken soup without the chicken, and weak broth at that.

That story is a symptom of the strange way in which biblical religion is understood today. And yet some understand quite well. If you google together the five words *truck, boat, helicopter, flood* and *God*, you will find more than 150,000 instances of a joke that runs something like this: There once was a man in a flood in the upper Mississippi valley, whose neighbors came (twice!) in trucks, once in a rowboat, and once in a helicopter to save him. He declined each time, saying God would rescue him; he had faith. The waters rose, and he drowned. In heaven, he asked the Lord why He didn't save him. God said to him, "I sent you two pickup trucks, a boat, and a helicopter; why didn't you get in?"

The two understandings of how God acts are poles apart, yet the first one seems to vex culture today. We can't quite make it to the second. How did we get to this state of affairs? And how much have we forgotten about biblical religion? How much did we never really know about biblical religion?

This book is about those questions.

1.2 Remedies

If the purpose of biblical religion is not to get you out of the pains of life, then what *is* its purpose? Do we simply assume that some other way to minimize pain and maximize pleasure is to be substituted in its stead? Is that what life is all about? Is it so obvious that it goes without saying? All "religions" are strategies, that is, they are ways to get what you want? To say that would assume you actually *can* get what you want (and if you fail, you lose big). It also says that if you *can't* get what you want, then something is deeply wrong with life and the world. Or at least, if you can't want something both worthwhile and accessible, then something is badly wrong.

Life without disappointments we can all imagine—but it doesn't seem to happen. Those who think they can avoid the disappointments should, I suppose, just try to find better remedies than biblical religion. Biblical religion is not likely to offer much help.

If we are left with a world full of pains, then a second question arises. What do you do with a world full of disappointments? Can they bring any good? Or are they barren? Is life to be valued only in the parts that have no disappointments, no pains? Do the hard parts poison the rest of life? Is the good to be sought somewhere other than in this life?

Try another possibility. Suppose that the anecdote about the radio evangelist has it wrong—Christianity is not about getting out of the pains of life. What if Christianity is about finding good in all of life, pains included?

Grant that the pains of life are real. Might it be possible to integrate all of life, pains included, into something good? Might it be possible to make sense of life as a whole so that it is good? Might it be possible to say that life in this world is good? Suppose that it is. That would indeed be good news—but it would come at a fearful price. The pains can destroy you well before your natural life-span, and in any case, we all die in the end.

This is the possibility I would like to explore. I think that many people within the communities of biblical religion today inherit an intuition that really does affirm life as good, in full view of its pains. And many outside of those communities would like such a vision, and think they cannot get it from present-day Christianity or Judaism. The idea *that* life might be good, taken as a whole, pains included, I have explored in other books, and they would be a good place to begin. The interested reader may consult *By the Waters of Naturalism* and *Unwelcome Good News*. *The Waters of Naturalism* explored only part of the present difficulties of theology, namely, the confusions that lead people to look for God in nature, as just one more natural phenomenon among other natural phenomena. It looked at very little of the history by which we got to where we are now. *Unwelcome Good News* looked only at the bare commitment to embrace all of life as good, with very little background or development of that commitment. The central commitment to affirming life will certainly emerge here also, but it will appear historically, as the tale unfolds.

1.3 Stuck in History

We seem to be in a predicament, and the jokes we began with are just hints of how bad things are. We won't understand our problems until we know *how* we got here. It is a *historical* predicament. We need to unravel our history. If that can't be done, or if history promises only trouble, confusion, and no way forward, then our situation is indeed grim. It could be that we are condemned to repeat history if we don't understand it, and maybe even if we do understand it. If that were to happen, some remedies outside of history would be needed.

As it happens, what is known is somewhat encouraging. Biblical scholars turned to history more than two hundred years ago, and they saw how big a role it plays in the story of the Bible. We need to understand history to make sense of the Bible. Big as history was in the estimation of the biblical scholars in the nineteenth century, I don't think people realized quite how big it really is until Mircea Eliade in the twentieth century looked at religions that don't know history, or don't want to have anything to do with history. Then he saw that for the aboriginal religions the world over, history is terror, if it is seen at all. Nature is orderly, human life is part of nature, and your job is to fit into nature naturally. For a hunter-gatherer society, without writing or iron, this is a pretty good strategy for dealing with life. But if you live in an agricultural society, with iron and writing, things begin to be different. There are new problems, and the old solutions don't work any more. We shall come to the transition in a few pages.

But for now, Eliade's words are enough: "history is terror." History is disorder, history is uncontrollable, history is what the original nature religions can't handle. History is evil. History means in all likelihood that you are living in the boonies, you have no power over the course of history, and when you come to the attention of folks in the big city, it is because they want to rob you, enslave you, or kill you. And what if you are lucky today, not even rich, just lucky enough to get by comfortably? You could lose it all tomorrow.

Nevertheless, a few people do sometimes seek good in human life in history, and they do so in full view of its pains, not just because they happen to be enjoying their fifteen minutes of fame and imperial glory. Look at the pains, in Edward Hobbs's survey of them: You can be embarrassed, caught red-handed, *exposed*. You can be frustrated, unable to get what you want, unable to do what you want. You're up against *limitation*. You may be stuck with neighbors in *need* whose demands on your time, effort, and resources will put a serious crimp in your plans for a picnic.

Suffice it to say that if you come clean before exposure, you will get freedom, freedom from living concealment. Exposure may be very costly, so one asks, is that freedom worth it? If you embrace limitation, you will find creativity. Sounds hard when you are about to be destroyed, but you can, at a minimum, offer a blessing to someone near to you. If you open your heart to your neighbor, you will get fellowship and community. We shall see these three pains again, for they are the key to unravelling the predicament of Christianity in the modern world.

These three pains come in many ways, to individuals, to communities, to entire cultures and traditions. They come to Christianity as a whole in ways that are not too hard to spot. Exposure threatens in the discovery that things didn't happen exactly as the Bible says they did. In short, it comes any time that history reveals that tradition was wrong. For tradition sought to portray the religion we know as Christianity as unspotted, started by God himself, and the only way to salvation. History shows plenty of spots, it can't find God, and it shows lots of alternatives to every religion, Christianity included. It shows rabbinic Judaism—at a minimum—as co-heir of the tradition passed on from before the time of Jesus. (So Christianity has no monopoly!)

Christian tradition sought to portray itself as not just true, but true "absolutely," without reference to time or place. History shows otherwise, and opens the door to cultural and religious relativity. That doesn't mean nothing means anything, but it does mean that all religions—Christianity included—are products of their own time and circumstances and historical origins. Relativity shows itself in the encounter with other religions and other cultures, an encounter that has become casual and is available on an everyday basis in a world where people fly to another continent one day and back the next. Religious pluralism is a fact of life in the modern world. When an instructor in world religions in a college not far from me stopped, perplexed about what Jains do at one particular passage in their lives, six Jains raised their hands in class with an answer. Even "minor" religions are represented in cosmopolitan cities today. Your neighbors probably don't belong to your religion, perhaps to none at all. "Religion" is a voluntary activity.

History, relativity, and pluralism are respectively kinds of exposure, limitation, and need. In history, we meet the truth about our own tradition. In relativity, we meet cultural limitation on what we can do and also the fact that our culture is the author of its own religion (simply because other cultures disagree). We have no proof for our religion, and we are left holding the bag when others disagree. In pluralism, we meet other cultures and other religions who also are engaged in the business of trying to make sense of the cosmos. We all do so in face of eventual and certain death. They would like us to validate *their* cosmos, instead of them validating ours. For we are all lonely before death and chaos, we need each other, but we all think we need the other people to validate our own religion.

Let us assume that in history we meet a truth that offers freedom, rather than fatal accusations that make biblical religion unredeemable. Assume that in relativity, we meet an opening to creativity, rather than nihilistic relativism. And assume that in religious pluralism we meet an opportunity for community instead of inescapable strife. These blessings will take time to find and assimilate—generations. History of religions is not known nearly as well as we would like. Relativity is usually something we can't understand very well, somewhat like the water that the fish will be the last to discover. And pluralism means getting to know other cultures and other religions far better than we do now. There is too much work to do—haste would be reckless. But it is possible to get a better idea of how we got to where we are.

Chapter 2

So What Really Did Happen?

2.1 Starting Points

The story begins with a peek at the end, which is a little bit familiar. The end of the story is about how the Christian world came apart, and about how the Bible was put together. Then we shall just go over the history of Israelite religion and the history of the writing of the Bible, saving the evidence for that story for later, in section 7.4.

"Religion," by which is usually meant Christianity, has been feeling perplexed since the eighteenth century, and the perplexity has been accelerating since the nineteenth. All hell broke loose in the twentieth century. Some issues have been different for Jews, because of the history in Europe in these centuries. But while Jews have not had the luxury of contemplating biblical religion in relative peace and security, there has still been a lot of overlap with Christian confusions.

In the beginning was Charles Darwin. He stands out as the icon of trouble, certainly the best known. For he supposedly proved that the world (or at least life in it) was not created, but instead evolved naturally. And evolution was not nice but nasty, the strong eating the weak. To call it "survival of the fittest" is to put a moral appearance on what was a gory, bloody mess. To call the survivors more deserving is pretentious. Really, it was just the survival of the survivors. (And I do not make an exception for human evolution; we were the same way—as far as biology is concerned.)

In any case, the "traditional" explanation of the creation of life has been discredited for many in this century. With the epic of creation went the ethic of creation, an ethic in which people have a kind of moral obligation to one another that they do not have if human life is just part of nature. Some have defied Darwin and evolution without a qualm. Some have admitted evolution as science and continued to believe in creation as theology. For better or for worse, they have not worried much about being consistent. (This may not be a bad thing; there's nothing wrong with admitting that you don't know enough to find a consistent position. You just proceed with common sense in various parts of life and leave consistency to those who can find it—later.) And many others rejoiced to embrace the apparent message of Darwin, that human life really is just a part of nature, nature is all there is, and so your job is to fit into nature naturally.

In the popular imagination, that's about as far as the story goes.

History tells us there was more, a lot more. Troubles began long before Darwin, with the issue of "miracles," with David Hume. He articulated a case against "miracles" in the 1700s. His logic in regard to miracles has attracted a lot of flak, some of it justified. But I think his *instincts* were pretty sensible about "miracles." I put the word in scare-quotes because the idea of what a miracle was had changed in the century and a half from 1600 to 1750. I would surmise that the change happened in the light of the new sciences. For in the light of science, the world of nature looked lawful in a way that it had not before. Nature has always been the realm of order, but the depth of order was thoroughly radicalized by the new sciences. It is enough to say that the "miracles" as they were newly read in the eighteenth century had lost a lot of plausibility. If Hume was the voice of the complaint, he spoke for his age.

More interesting and less known were the changes in the way

biblical texts and biblical history were read. People began to suspect multiple authors in parts of the Bible that were previously thought to come from single hands (or single pens). The first five books, formerly thought to come from Moses, looked suspiciously like the work of many editors. Suspicion in the eighteenth century turned to confidence in the nineteenth, and people thought they knew who the editors were, what they contributed, and roughly when. In the popular imagination, not only are we no longer created (because evolved), but also, the Bible was not written by God (because it was written by human authors).

How could you believe the Bible? Why should you? After all, the Bible was just made up by people long ago. Ignorant people, too, judging by modern standards. We are alone in the universe, and the universe doesn't care about us. Whether this message was embraced or defied, it was the plain appearance of things.

Yet there was more—more changes in the way the past was understood by historians. A lot more. For when the scoffers found enough to impeach the Bible, they quit and went elsewhere. But there were plenty of biblical scholars who were faithful in their own way, who persisted, as if to ask, "All right, if the Bible wasn't written the way we thought it was, how *was* it written?" What did happen? If Israelite religion was not what we thought from our "literal" reading of the Bible, what was it? How did it all get started? And out of that questioning came a world quite transformed. It is often said that only now, in the twentieth century, have biblical scholars been free to use the kind of scholarship on biblical questions that is standard in secular history. But in fact, the techniques of questioning were often first developed by biblical scholars, working in obscurity (or under the ban of excommunication) and then later turned to secular questions. Serious textual criticism of Plato started in the nineteenth century, well after textual criticism of the Bible. Modern biblical criticism started in the eighteenth century, but had its roots in the seventeenth. In a way, this is not at all surprising: people develop new methods for the history they care most about, and turn to lesser questions only afterward. We come to this part of the story in section 7.4.

These scholars were very courageous, for they risked everything their inherited faith could give them for the sake of the truth. Nothing like it has happened in the sciences—not in this century or in any other. Galileo was a martyr, in a sense (he was prosecuted, but not killed), but he never risked finding *in his own mind* that science was just all wrong. Liberal biblical scholars of the nineteenth century risked exactly that. It is hard to tell to what degree Galileo's science was the center of his basic life orientation, the center of his cosmos. He was, after all, a faithful Catholic. And he was an Aristotelian philosopher, if a deviant Aristotelian by the fashionable standards in his part of Italy. So if the risk for Galileo is hard to gauge, the risk for the nineteenth-century biblical scholars is not. They knew they were risking an entire worldview. (I don't want to glorify them unduly; rather than clear-sighted, they were often muddle-headed. They could not see what we see, though that may add to their courage, even if it undermines any simple myths about them.)

As things turned out, what they found was quite different from the received "traditions," but it was also *not* just nonsense, superstition, magic or delusions. The shape of biblical religion stands out with a clarity after critical history that it never had before. Their work started to come together in the synthesis created by Julius Wellhausen in the nineteenth century, who collected together the theories about the editing of the Common Documents, the documents that are shared in common by the Church and the Synagogue. He can stand as an icon for them all. We shall come to him and to his work in due time.

2.2 Before the Beginning

As it happens, the story of religion *before* the Bible has changed in recent years. We know enormously more now than people did a hundred or two hundred years ago, but the popular myths about mankind's original religions haven't changed much since long before the Enlightenment.

The stereotypical account of the original religions was simply that people worshipped many gods, and they made visible images of those gods, usually as statues. Both the arithmetic (more than one) and the visible images were forbidden in the Bible, and that's all you need to know about pre-biblical religion. Pre-biblical religion was just the "bad" religions of the Old Testament.

Today, things look different, and biblical religion itself will look a lot different when its background in the original religions of the area can be appreciated. Progress began with archaeology, the digging up of ruins in the ancient Near East: Greece, Asia Minor, Mesopotamia, Syria, and Egypt. What had been just the history in the Bible and a few Greek and Roman historians was actually dug up, found, put on display in museums, turned into a spectacle, given if not flesh and blood at least pottery and stone remains. And often texts as well. Stones had engravings on them, then parchments were found in libraries, and papyrus manuscripts were preserved in the dry climate of the Egyptian desert. Many texts were recovered, first from Egypt and Mesopotamia, then from Syria. It took some work to decode them—often the languages they were written in had been lost for millennia. The languages were recovered. The ancient near east took on a detail it had lost for twenty or thirty centuries.

Then attention turned from the background of the Bible to the original religions everywhere else. Out of the nineteenth century guesses about religion came some fairly simple generalizations in the twentieth century. Aboriginal religion exhibits variations on a few themes. The central idea, as we would see it from the outside, is that the world is just nature, nature is all there is, and your job is to fit into nature naturally. Harmony of nature is the ultimate good. Disorder in nature is the definition of evil, and disturbance of nature is the definition of sin (or substitute for sin, if you prefer). From the inside, of course, there is just "the world," and it is what we would call *nature* only because we have a concept of nature in contrast, say, to history.

Without writing, you can't remember enough detail to keep history, you can't remember enough to protect yourself from stereotypes. Pre-literate societies had (and have) narratives enough, but they are narratives that can be memorized easily. The narrative works itself out with a logic fore-ordained in its starting point by the logic of nature. There are no details you would want to argue over. The characterizations are clean and unproblematic, even of people who get themselves into trouble.

Without iron, you can't build a multinational empire, and so you don't have much contact with other cultures. You don't get an idea of how big the world is, or of the variety in it. You don't travel far (Bellah).

So we could start the story this way:

In the beginning there were hunter-gatherers, who lived very close to nature. They sought to fit into nature naturally. (You would too, if you were one of them. How could you do otherwise?) Nature is what is orderly and regular, but the nature of the wild is orderly in a disorderly way. It is very much like a living organism, not always predictable unless you stay close to nature. And stay close they did. You listen carefully, look hard, remember how things were last year at this time, ten years ago at this time, when the hard weather came, how the animals traveled, when they came, when they didn't. You are in a sort of give-and-take with nature; it is open and free, even in its orderliness. You have to listen and watch. Nature feeds you, but it is alive, to be respected but not to be manipulated. You ask, and it may give, it may not. You give in return. You respect nature—and thank it.

Food can be scarce. You go out alone and hungry into the wild. Pretty soon the animals come and talk to you. They tell you what to do. The people who could do that were known as *shamans* in north Asia, and that word has been borrowed for the role of speaker-to-animals on any continent. Actually, he (or she, there are women shamans too) was as much a hearer as speaker. When your life is not fitting into nature naturally, the way you would like, you go to the shaman, and he helps set things right.

Things changed some, as I have said, when agriculture came. Farmers can feed more people, and then you have more children, and the population rises. Soon agriculture became a necessity. There was no going back to the old hunter-gatherer ways. Farmers have a different "life-style"—the modern word says it better than any other can. They need regularity in nature even more than their hunter-gatherer ancestors did. For if the rains don't come on time, the crops will not grow. If you don't plant on time, the crops won't grow. You need a calendar, and for that, you need astronomy, and for that, you need some arithmetic. (Quite a lot, by modern grade-school standards!) The center of your life turns around the seasons and the weather, and they are *supposed* to be regular—much more regular even than the ways of the animals for the hunters in times gone by. The hunters were supposed to be a small perturbation on the ecosystems they lived in, because there weren't very many of them. They were supposed to fit into the harmony of nature without disrupting it, but they did not. When humans arrived in the Americas, they hunted roughly three quarters of the large game animal species to extinction. But with farming, things changed even more. With larger populations, a bad year could mean famine, major disaster. The land itself began to look differently under cultivation.

Basic life orientation is pretty simple in such a world, even when it was sophisticated. You need the cycles to come on time. But there is enough variation in the earth's orbit, the sun's radiation, and just in the randomness of the weather, so that things don't always come on time. You want to be in control; after all, the crops are planted under your control, and it would be nice if you could control the rain and the sun as well. You do try, for what it is worth. You cajole, you plead, you bribe. Sometimes the sun and the rain listen, sometimes they don't.

"Basic life orientation" is the term I would prefer to use in place of "religion." It is simpler and clearer, and it applies to everybody, not just latter-day biblical religionists. To be fussy, you have to add some recognition and intention to basic life orientation for it to qualify as a religion, but the idea is clear. *Religio* in Latin means something close to discipline, after all, and that's what recognition and intention do—they supply discipline.

Life in the first agricultural societies was very much oriented to nature, just as it had been for the shamanisms of the earlier hunter-gatherer cultures. But there were some differences. These people could write, and we have what they wrote, so we hear a little about how they viewed their world. The Enuma Elish, Gilgamesh, and other stories like them are the classic Western in-the-beginning stories. We have them on a few clay tablets from the library of Ashurbanipal at Nineveh. Gilgamesh is known also from much older sources; it probably dates to about 2000 BCE.

The Babylonian Creation Epic tells a story of a great flood. It begins with the beginning of the gods, a battle between Marduk and Tiamat, and the creation of the universe and mankind. Apsu personifies the fresh waters, and Tiamat the salty deep, storm and chaos. Soon there are more gods, Marduk among them, and soon enough, they are quarreling. Marduk kills Tiamat and creates the world out of parts of Tiamat's body. It is a story of good and evil, of a struggle, with the eventual victory of good over evil. This story and others like it were common lore in the ancient near east, and when the Bible was put together, a somewhat modified version appears in the first chapter of Genesis. It's worth noting that in the Enuma Elish, the world is not obviously good at the beginning, but is made so only by a struggle. In Genesis 1, it is all good, right at the beginning, a difference we shall return to.

These stories were told to make sense of a very particular world, Babylon and its near neighbors. The heros are local, and the Enuma Elish celebrates Babylon. Part of the annual creation festival was a reading of the story of creation. For creation in Babylon was a way to reset the clock, to restore order, to bring things back to the order they had in the beginning, after Marduk's victory over Tiamat. Creation is not (as we shall see later on) the beginning of history but the model for nature. Here, time is cyclical, the cycles of time repeat over the years and centuries, and that order was profoundly comforting. It makes life predictable, and what is predictable is reliable.

What disturbs that order is profoundly discomforting—and therein lies the experience of evil in the life of the ancient Near East.

2.3 Archetypes

Look at the way people tell stories in world-affirming nature religions. Enough of them survive. They have been recorded, written down, scouted out by anthropologists, linguists, students of myth. This kind of folklore has survived far longer than you would expect in districts where literacy was infrequent. And that is the key: for with literacy, people can write down what happens from one day to the next, and those texts will live on. Those records will correct faulty memories, and testify against overactive imaginations. Indeed, with literacy, the older kind of memory tends to atrophy and die out.

Where writing is scarce or unavailable, a different sort of memory is required. You can only remember stories that have some simple thread holding them together. A story has to have a life of its own to be remembered.

In pre-literate societies, you can only remember a few simple *types* of stories. They are called "archetypes," and an archetype is a kind of master-story. It is like a script: you can change the names of the characters, even the time and place, but you can't change the action much. An archetype is just How Things Work. Things always work like one or another archetype. Stories that don't fit the archetypes are bent and stretched until they do.

This kind of memory gives you something intensely comforting, profoundly reassuring. For your life can now be fitted into archetypes. You are not stuck in chaos bereft of meaning when things go wrong, when a relationship with other people is in trouble, when you don't know how things will turn out. You know what can happen, the meanings are already given for you.

And when things do go wrong, there are remedies. For the shaman (in the original hunter-gatherer societies) or the priest (in the later, sophisticated agricultural version) can restore the natural order. Indeed, the new-year's festival is designed to do just that, for the society as a whole.

In this sort of a world, myth plays a pivotal role, for myth depicts the original state of harmony with nature. It was, as I have said, a harmony won at some cost, for the creation was a contest of good and evil. Nevertheless, that original time can be restored.

When things can't be set right just now, when people die in fortuitous accidents, archetypes can give the misfortune some meaning. There is a famous example of how a prosaic accident was turned into an archetypical story in the recent past, early in the twentieth century in Romania. Mircea Eliade retells it in *Cosmos and History* (pp. 44-45). Constantin Brailoiu, an anthropologist and folklorist, chanced to come upon the story. It was a wedding-day tragedy in which the groom fell over a cliff and was remembered in lyric and heroic terms, with considerable embellishment of fact. But as it happened, the bride was still alive, and with clear memory. It was possible to observe the transformation of fact into archetype a bare few years after it actually happened. The archaic mind, even in its modern surviving form in rural Maramures, fitted the events into an archetype that could be remembered easily *and with meaning*. Meaningless suffering is unbearable—and indeed, unrememberable.

I presume that when you face a crisis in the near future in such a society, you go to a shaman. The shaman reviews for you the available archetypical stories, and tells you what you can do to bring about the more desirable of them. In any case, your only possibilities are to play one of the roles given in them, even though you don't know which archetype will actually be realized. In effect, the archetype plays itself out in you, or the archetype just plays you; you don't play it. This is an understanding of human action that has some noticeable differences from the ideas of human action in the modern world.

2.4 The Beauty of Nature

Some features of aboriginal societies and their way of life should not be missed. It is not enough to say they lived close to nature. Nature for them had a richness and a texture that modern city-folk could easily miss.

The nineteenth century was the heyday of the British Empire. India was consolidated under British control, and much of Africa also. Australia came into its own. It was almost as if the British could for the first time sit back and take a longer look at what they had conquered. That century was also a time of considerable changes in religious outlook. "Atheism" in the eighteenth century was visible enough to be a scandal, but it was not widespread enough to be available to just anybody. Things were looser in the nineteenth century. It was the time of Charles Darwin, and *The Origin of Species* (1859) and *The Descent of Man* (1871) put human origins in an entirely new light. It was the time of Karl Marx, who accused western economics of being a tool of exploitation and also of concealing its own real workings. In Germany, Ludwig Feuerbach had proposed that religion was just a "projection," i.e., a writing of human features on the cosmos at large. Biblical scholars were beginning to unravel the early history of Israel. How much that work was noticed outside of universities (apart from a few scandals) I do not know. It was a time when open lectures fed a public curiosity that had an unprecedented appetite and horizon of interest.

In this Victorian milieu a self-educated scholar named Edward Burnett Tylor became the first professor of anthropology at Oxford. He and his student, James G. Fraser, questioned every person returning from the far corners of the world. Their explanation of religion is not well regarded now, but we should not be too patronizing toward an outmoded theory. For it was a radical improvement over the tacit folk-explanation of other religions as just variations on the "bad" religions of the Old Testament.

Tylor thought that for primitive peoples (his term), everything in nature had a soul, and the soul, or *anima* in Latin, was what made it do its thing in nature. If you wanted it to do something for you, you just asked it to. This was to explain primitive religion as *animism*. Tylor thought that animism was succeeded by religion, meaning Judaism, Christianity, and Islam. And religion would be succeeded by science.

Notice that his use of the term "religion" is quite different from mine: I take religion to be someone's basic life orientation—whatever that may be. Tylor, Fraser, and many after them until the present day use the term "religion" to mean just Christianity and things like it. But for them, science was to be the center of a basic life orientation. They are entitled to their choice of basic life orientation—at least for now, when I am speaking as just a historian of religions. Later, and speaking for myself, much as I like the sciences (I am myself a physicist), I would have to say that the sciences belong not *quite* at the exact center of things.

There is an old saying that truth proceeds more readily from error than from confusion. If so, then Tylor and Fraser's theories were the first modern errors, and very useful ones, too. For they could be corrected. The folk notion that religions before the Bible were just idol-worship was not even corrigible; there just wasn't enough of a theory there.

Since Tylor and Fraser, things have changed some, but there are some general themes. From the nineteenth until well into the twentieth century, people assumed that religion was one department or activity of life among others, and they sought to identify what its peculiar interest was. Some thought it was gods, until religions turned up that had no gods. People found cultures, and human lives in them, that had no visible gods, but did have elaborate rituals and other trappings of "religion" in the West.

In the first half of the twentieth century, the work of Tylor and Fraser was turned into something that could be tested in the field. Mircea Eliade was not the only scholar at this stage of the study of religion, but he is the most notorious, and he trained a generation of scholars after him. He grew up in Romania, and studied briefly in India. In the late 1950s, he came to the University of Chicago. When he arrived, I believe there were only a very few chairs in religious studies in America. Fifteen years later, there were thirty, half occupied by his students.

His approach was not to try to reduce all religions, or even all "primitive" religions to some simple explanation. His method in studying religion was to go out and listen to people in their own words, to try to get a sense of how their world looked to them, to try to get inside their world. This allows you some space to get to know another religion. Judging it or explaining it away can wait until later, if you care to do that at all. It made it possible to like the world's religions as only getting to know them can. No wonder religious studies departments flourished.

2.5 Society as Nature

A society whose highest goal is to fit into nature naturally still faces pains, some of its own making. The management—kings, priests, other leaders—has a place that mirrors the structure of nature. Their roles are supposedly given in the natural order. And the natural cannot be questioned. It just *is*. It is pre-given. It cannot be changed. It cannot be challenged. At least that is the way things were supposed to be.

Later, when the civilizations of Egypt, Mesopotamia, Greece, and Asia Minor came in frequent and casual contact with each other, they could not help noticing that the natural order of things was a little different in each land. Nevertheless, the goals in these societies remained pretty much the same. The rulers were supposed to preserve order, and provide for the common good. In fact, the king *was* the highest good in the land; his subjects were privileged to be subjected to him. To question that subjection would have endangered the order of the cosmos. No amount of suffering at the hands of the government was too great a price to pay to preserve that cosmic order. Meaningful suffering was infinitely preferable to meaningless existence—with or without immediate suffering.

There is a very simple consequence. When the government is sacred, you can't criticize the government. This may seem odd to people who have grown up in Western democracies, where criticizing the government is one of the most common pastimes. Yet we know things can be different, for we have heard tales enough from Stalinist Russia and other such places. Alexander Solzhenitsyn can stand as witness. But there is an important difference between Stalin and Pharaoh (for it is Pharaoh that we shall be most interested in). Stalin ruled by terror, and terror is necessary when the people know that things could be different, and things are not right as they stand. Pharaoh had no such need—he was a god, Egyptian society was a model of the cosmic order, and so his view of how to rule Egypt had to be right, *necessarily* right. Other arrangements were unthinkable; terror was not needed.

Problems arise at several places. Governments that can't be criticized can't be stopped from mistreating their subjects. That we have seen. Problems of another sort arise simply from trying to copy nature. For nature (at least nature before man) is an ecosystem and not a society. The difference might not seem like much, but it is. For in an ecosystem, different animals and different species live in relations of mutual exploitation. Cordial if possible (it's called symbiosis), predatory if necessary. Ruthless always. What this works out to is tribalism, and another name for tribalism is racism. We'll cooperate if it's to my advantage, and otherwise not. That's assuming I am the stronger party.

Pains happen in other ways, too. For although human society as part of nature was supposed to be orderly, it often was not. Natural disasters are only the perturbations that come to mind first. Your neighbors may come to visit, and overstay their invitation. Perhaps they are not nice neighbors. Or you may come to the attention of the authorities. Or new ways may come along, as they did with new technologies from time to time. First the finer things of life: beer, wine, bread, pottery, alphabetic writing, then copper and bronze. And gold, for ornaments. What was the old order doesn't work anymore, and the new has come in its place. Nature is not supposed to be that way, nature is supposed to be stable and enduring.

Remember that in the aboriginal nature religions, the purpose of it all was to affirm human life in this world, and the way to do that was to fit into nature naturally. When life beyond nature becomes visible, there is always the possibility that sooner or later, somewhere, sometime, someone will try to affirm life as it is, in all its disorder, even though it doesn't fit into nature as it should.

In practice, two things are needed for this to happen. The less important is iron technology, for it only enables people to travel enough so that they get a sense of how big the world is, how different things can be. The first people to do a historical religion didn't even have iron themselves. Much the more important is writing. With writing, stories can be recorded in texts, and the texts can withstand the impulse to transform the past into archetypes. If there had been writing (enough writing; there must have been some) in that village in Romania that Constantin Brailoiu visited, the tragedy of love could not have been turned into a legend. The texts would have stood as witness against overactive imaginations.

When writing is available, many things become possible that were not before. You are not forced to reduce narratives to archetypes. You can go back and ask whether the written records really tell what happened. And you can create new interpretations of the past. You have an openness that was unprecedented, and perhaps not entirely welcome. This is life in history.

And sooner or later, some people did attempt to affirm human life in history. It did not happen at the center of an "advanced" civilization, where you would expect it, with lots of metal technology and abundant written archives. It happened among the out-people, the marginalized.

In the next two chapters, I would like to tell the story of Israelite religion, from the days of David and Solomon to the end in the first century, when the Romans destroyed the Temple and drove the Jews out of the land of Israel. After that, we will see how Christians and Jews sorted things out after the disasters, and how the ancient world was transformed by stages into the modern.

We take the history of Israel together with its written history, with how the texts were put together in Genesis to Deuteronomy (known as the Pentateuch) and Joshua to 2 Kings (known as the Former Prophets). For now, we begin with the simple version, just as beginning physics students learn classical mechanics in its simplest form, even though physics has long since shown that Newtonian mechanics is "wrong."

The story of the texts has a name, the "Documentary Hypothesis." We shall not come to its discovery until section 7.4, when our own story gets to the modern world, so it would be good to say a little about it at the start. Recent doubts about the documentary hypothesis make sense only after one knows what the doubts are about, the doubts are technical, and have not commanded widespread assent. In brief, the documentary hypothesis is the conjecture that the Pentateuch passed through the hands of four editors, known by the letters J, E, D, and P. We come to them in the history of the Israelite kingdoms because in the original form of the hypothesis, each editor responded to political and theological problems of his own time.

The trouble is that the documentary hypothesis has never really been stable, but it has never been decisively overturned for some other, better theory. Scholars have the most confidence about D and P, which stand out distinctively, while J and E are sometimes hard to separate from each other and from miscellaneous lesser traditions. In the end, it is like a low-resolution picture that stubbornly refuses to come into focus, and no amount of massaging the data can fix that. In addition, the conjectured dates for the four sources have never commanded universal agreement. If each source was not a single edition of the texts but a multi-century tradition in its own right, it is not clear what it would even mean to speak of dates for the sources.

Confidence in the theory is not what it once was, but there is no better, and one thing really does survive from the documentary hypothesis: in the historical and legal books of the Old Testament, we are looking at the contributions of many authors, editors, points of view, and traditions. These are composite texts. In that assessment, confidence has increased, not decreased. With that caution in mind, let's have a look at a simplified version of the history. The history of Israel is interleaved with the history of the texts.

Chapter 3

The First History

3.1 King Solomon's Problem

When the dust had settled, the turning point was clearly the Exodus from Egypt, when a few dozen families of migrant laborers escaped from slavery in the cosmopolitan civilization. (The numbers in modern translations of the Bible, "six hundred thousand," are not really believable.) The events were ignored by the Egyptians but life-changing for the ones who got out. Moses the shaman does a very un-shamanly thing and leads his people out of nature and into history. The story of the Exodus is told (briefly) in *By The Waters of Naturalism* (chapter 6, "Here's the Tell").

There is a better way to retell the story here. For it was not written down in a form that survived until much later, in the time of David and Solomon or a little after. Instead of retelling the story of Moses, look at the story of Solomon. For it was at the time of Solomon or thereabouts (at the earliest) that the story of Moses was first collected and written down in anything like the form we have it today.

The texts may be considerably younger than the time of Solomon. In any case, *they* thought their lives were changed long before in the Exodus, for they said so. And the Exodus does not have the obviously fictional texture that Jonah or Daniel or Esther do. The history is impossible to recover with confidence, but ask yourself this question: There was constant traffic of subject peoples in and out of Egypt, sometimes happy, sometimes not; it is always that way with metropolitan or imperial powers. But what are the chances that *no one* who left Egypt under disagreeable circumstances ended up as part of the later Israelite society? Not great. So if we can assume only this minimalist account of the Exodus, we can get on with our own reconstruction. Things are on comparatively more solid ground when we come to the time of Solomon.

Solomon, as the story unfolds in 1 and 2 Samuel, up through 1 Kings 12, was not the oldest son of his father. And his father was not the first king in Israel. Solomon had gotten the throne through questionable palace politics. His father had gotten the throne at the expense of the first king, Saul. And even Saul did not have a clear title to the throne, if you can read between the lines, for many thought there should not even be a king at all. Solomon had a triple problem.

To start the story, we have to look a little earlier than Solomon himself. In the beginning were the judges, and the judges ruled Israel quite well enough, settling disputes and leading occasional wars against the locals. This was in a time when the Israelites had come into a modest piece of land that wasn't worth much to anyone else but them. It was on the road between one big empire and another, but both empires were happy to leave them alone for a few centuries. We call that land by their name, Israel, but for them it was the land of Canaan, the land where Canaanites lived. The Philistines arrived around 1200 BCE from the sea. Other people later called the land Palestine, named for the Philistines.

In any case, the Israelites were not without problems. They did not have iron technology (the Philistines did), and that made fighting hard for them. The Philistines tended to win.

More interesting, the Israelites had a somewhat strange religion. It was originally a world-affirming nature religion, just like everybody else's, but it was slowly becoming something different. They were a group of a dozen and a half tribes, each with a separate identity. They had traditions enough, to be sure. Though there were well over a dozen tribes, their traditions spoke of a baker's dozen. In many ways, they were much like their neighbors, for the literature that survives was a literature shared with their neighbors. In some ways, they were more primitive than their neighbors. For the neighbors had temples, with gods in them, and the neighbors had iron technology, and a higher standard of living. But the people we are interested in still remembered their nomadic ways in the desert, and to some extent still lived that way. They did not lack sacred objects. One such, more memorable than most, was a sort of box with some stones and other heirlooms in it. And those stones may have had some writing on them, a witness of older traditions. It's hard to tell, because the records are so close to legends at this stage. They lacked, and lacked on purpose, any statue of the deity. At least that's the way their somewhat idealistic literary executors have it centuries later.

It was odd, in later hindsight, that they had judges instead of kings. A judge was someone who was full of charismatic energy, who could lead the people on a short-term basis. In between wars, the judge was supposed to, well, judge—set things right. Settle disputes, that sort of thing. The judge was supposed to act for the god or gods. It's not entirely clear how they thought of the gods at this stage. In some ways, all the local gods were just names for one god. Tradition had it that this god had brought these people out of Egypt many years before. Subject peoples entered and occasionally left Egypt. These people thought it was a big thing—they had not expected to escape from Egypt at all. We shall soon see what became of that tradition.

In any case, there was some discontent in the period of the judges. The trouble was, having informal judges was not a very effective form of organization.

We should note by the way that there were still plenty of people among the Israelites who were more or less like shamans of older days. They had visions and ecstatic trances, they danced together in groups, and they sometimes presided over animal sacrifices. Eating meat was not the routine commonplace we know today, but a special occasion. These people remembered much of the aboriginal nature religions in which to eat an animal was to receive a gift, a gift to be shared, something for which one should be grateful, both because meat could be scarce, and also because the animal gave its life for its human masters.

Sometimes a judge was also a sort of shaman. One such was named Samuel. These Israelites were not doing too badly, but they thought they could do better. So they asked Samuel to give them a king. Their neighbors had kings, and kings seemed to be better commanders in war than the judges were. They could plan further ahead, and organize people better.

Samuel and the people went back and forth, Yes, we want a king one day, No, we don't want a king the next. Finally, God told Samuel (as the story has it) to give the people what they wanted. But in the other version, God was actually in favor of a king. Clearly, many people were not convinced, and events rattled from pillar to post for some years during the time of Saul and David. It wasn't clear who would be part of this kingdom, or whether they would be a part of it voluntarily, by joining, or involuntarily, by being forced.

And people remembered, even in the time of Solomon, how things had been a scant few years before. So Solomon had problems. A lot of people (a whole lot, as it turns out later) thought he shouldn't be king at all. They thought even less of his son and heir, Rehoboam.

This probably comes as a surprise to you. If you are like most people, you thought God just came down and said, "I think it's time to have a king," tried Saul, and when Saul didn't work out, fired him and chose David in his place. Solomon, of course, was the natural successor to David.

Solomon's problems were real. I would not have noticed them myself just by reading the text in 1 and 2 Samuel, but they are clear enough once pointed out. The treatment of Solomon is very delicate, and very complementary, until the end, when Rehoboam the son gets his fifteen minutes of fame. Rehoboam was not Solomon, Rehoboam could be criticized, but Rehoboam has been forgotten.

When German scholars were sorting through the texts they tumbled to what was going on. One Stefan Heym, an East German novelist, found their technical accounts and turned them into a novel. Heym had his motives, and he recognized parallels with his own time, for he was a Marxist, and in the 1940s, Joseph Stalin reigned as the father-founder of the Marxist order of society in Eastern Europe. Just as Solomon was the king who consolidated the Davidic empire, one that stretched from northeast Syria to the border of Egypt, and just as Solomon was a burden to his people, so also was Joseph Vissarionovich Dzhugashvili, known as the Man of Steel for short. If Solomon could be criticized indirectly in the Bible, perhaps people could see the truth about Stalin. I don't know whether modern readers heard Heym's point about Stalin or not, but his novel tells a lot about Solomon and David and the writing of the texts we have from their time, first of all the books of Samuel, but on a grander scale, the entire history from Genesis to Kings.

And so the story unfolds. Ethan the Ezrahite, an obscure scribe in the real Bible, in the novel becomes the editor hired to solve Solomon's triple problem of legitimacy. He is summoned to the court in Jerusalem, deftly made to understand that the consequences will be pleasant if he takes his masters' hints, and unpleasant indeed if he does not. There is a cabinet meeting. We see the powerful ministers assembled with Solomon to commission what is, to be candid, a propaganda piece. Stefan Heym's imagined title for the work is too good not to quote: "The One and Only True and Authoritative, Historically Correct and Officially Approved Report on the Amazing Rise, God-fearing Life, Heroic Deeds, and Wonderful Achievements of David the son of Jesse, King of Judah for Seven Years and of Both Judah and Israel for Thirty-three, Chosen of God, and Father of King Solomon." (*The King David Report*, p. 9) It was to settle all doubt and disbelief, end all controversy. What Ethan finds is not exactly what Solomon intended, and more stories than just one got into the text. Ethan has a scholar's conscience, and yet must satisfy (or fool) his royal master, and so many things are treated very delicately.

In real life, things were different in many details, but enough like Heym's imagination so that his novel tells us something very true about this biblical history. People often don't gather a history together until they need to use it, or until they are in danger of losing it. Records exist, in scraps and fragments, to be sure. There are always oral traditions about those fragments and where they came from, what was left out but was generally known. When an editor has to put it all together, that oral tradition gets written down. But an editor always has applications in mind in his own time, and those applications shape the narrative that results.

Royal injustice and oppression in Solomon's time are evident enough. What is not entirely obvious without some help is the degree to which the history, starting from the beginning, worked as a critique of Solomon.

3.2 Applied Exodus

The central texts, of course, are in Exodus, and the account of the Exodus governs all that comes after—and indeed, all that came before. They provide a standard, both in statute and example, by which later events are to be judged, and for which earlier events prepare.

Some of the texts must be much older than the time of Solomon, but the editorial arrangement comes from about his time. Students can find a list of books now lost that were still available then, just by looking in a concordance for the word "book," *sepher*. Nowadays, concordances are not as common as a flat-ascii text of the King James, which can be searched on a computer. The results are the same. Here are some of the titles: The book of Jashar, the book of the Wars of the Lord, the book of the Law of Moses, the book of the Just; and so on. The most cited were yet to be written, the Annals of the Kings of Judah and the Annals of the Kings of Israel. There must have been others, because we have embedded in the later text passages that feel and sound much older, such as the Song of the Sea (Exodus 15) and the Song of Deborah (Judges 5).

But these are only the most obvious. Even beginners can tell something is fishy in 1 Samuel, when the opinion regarding the proposed king changes from favorable to unfavorable about once a chapter, often on a chapter boundary. This story is called the "Succession Narrative," and it tells the story of how there came to be a king at all, and then how David got to be king. (That would solve two of Solomon's three problems). The Succession Narrative probably circulated as an independent document before it was integrated with the surrounding text later on. In fact, the Succession Narrative is just about what Stefan Heym had in mind when he made up the story of the "King David Report."

The Israelites, whoever they were before they came into the land of Canaan, were not entirely Canaanites. When they borrowed texts, they borrowed not from Canaanites but from places further north, like Ugarit, in present-day Syria, or Babylon, to the east. In one account (there are others), they didn't get along with the Canaanites very well, and didn't approve of the Canaanite city-folk ways. The Israelites were semi-nomads, with traditions of liberty and independence. The Canaanites were somewhat libertine, which is quite different from treasuring liberty. In fact, George Mendenhall remarked that the Canaanites had a "reputation for possessing a very low standard of morality, from which charge we could defend them only by assuming that they did not take their religion seriously."

In any case, the Israelites were doing well enough fending off the Canaanites, and even conquering them. It was the Sea Peoples, also known as the Philistines, who were causing the more serious problems. The Philistines had iron technology, and they could not so easily be defeated in war. And so the rough-and-ready amateur military organization of the Israelites was at its limits. It was natural to ask for a king; a king could organize people more effectively.

But these semi-nomads already had a king—their God. The manuscripts have a four-letter name, "YHWH," but how to pronounce that name is not entirely clear. In reverence, the name was read instead as the Lord, the Boss, "Adonai"; or just "THE NAME." Out of respect, we shall follow that tradition and mention but never use the Name. Even then, we mention it only where it is crucial to deciphering the editing of the texts, and then give it the German spelling, as a marker for the hazards in the Name. Usually, we shall print the Name as "THE NAME," as it is read in Hebrew. The tradition in English translations is "the LORD," which we may also use occasionally. The problem with a proper name is that it means the deity is disponible—anything that has a name is at human disposal, coming when called, going when dismissed. This God won't come when called, and may well come when not called. In any case, names are all of human invention, and so none can claim to be the "proper" Name. I do not know at what stage in the later history the faithful became reluctant to pronounce a name that was in all probability routinely pronounced like any other name in the early history.

This God was invisible, not to be imaged in stone or wood, not living in a house but traveling with them as they did, in tents—very much in keeping with the older days in which life was the gift of a wilderness that one could not control. Gratitude was the prime virtue, not agricultural engineering. And so when the people come to Samuel the judge and ask for a king, the Boss says to Samuel, It is not you they have rejected, but me. And a chapter later, it is not the people but the Boss himself who has concocted the idea of a king. And so on, back and forth, for a half-dozen chapters. Saul is king, then David, and David is crowned with mostly successes, though there are some problems in his own family. In the events that followed, Solomon ends up on the throne, though not without some palace politicking on the way. It all looks legitimate. Solomon's problems are solved.

But the predicted changes did come to pass. Forced labor for the king, high taxes, confiscation of lands by eminent domain, bureaucracy, and so on. (See the prediction in 1 Samuel 8, doubtless written after the fact by an editor who disapproved in hindsight, but with a recollection of some farsighted dissenters before the fact. (If there had not been at least a few vocal dissenters before the monarchy, the story wouldn't really make sense.)

The problem is clear enough: these people needed a government strong enough to discharge its necessary tasks in the changing world of the ancient Near East, but they also very much needed to be able to hold their government accountable. They needed to make it answer to the standards of the people, both standards inherited from their nomadic tradition and also standards of simple justice. And so the remedy came from tradition, the tradition of the Exodus. For in that tradition, the people had been enslaved by a government that put itself above criticism, and they had escaped, precisely so that both they as a people *and* their leaders could answer to the invisible Boss, Adonai, One who was just. That tradition could be summoned as a basis for criticizing Solomon.

But to be usable, that tradition had to be recollected, assembled from memories and maybe from a few written scraps.

3.3 J

Only a text would do, for only when you can hold a text under the King's nose can you say, "See, it says here." And so the tradition, to be useful, had to be written down. As just common memory, it could be dismissed or denied or twisted.

Things were somewhat more complicated than just one editor putting together The Story. There were at least two textual traditions, one from the south, in the kingdom of Judah, and one from the north, in the kingdom of Israel. For the monarchy had been split soon after Rehoboam came to the throne. The elders of the northern tribes said, in disgust at Rehoboam's program of accelerated taxes and oppression, "What share have we in the house of David?" And they left.

A man named Jeroboam became their first king. His first act was to turn Shechem into a fortified town, to serve as capital. More noticeably, he set up golden calves at the sanctuaries of Dan and Bethel, saying to the Israelites, "These are the gods who brought you out of Egypt." Bethel was in the middle of the hill-country north of Jerusalem; Dan was at the northern extremity of Israelite territory. (These two golden calves had no small part in the scandal in the texts, edited later than the Dan and Bethel images, about the golden calf that Aaron built on the way out of Egypt.)

This was the historical situation. As I said a moment ago, there were (at least) two textual traditions of the origins of these people, one from each kingdom. When scholars were confident about these things, the textual sources were known as "J" and "E." Today, there is much less confidence that things were as simple as that (see section 7.4), but at the beginning it is better to present the simple and earlier form of the theory. J and E did not originally stand for Judah and Ephraim (Ephraim was the largest tribe in the north), but that is not a bad way to help remember them. The two texts are named for their different names for God, "Jahweh" (as it was transliterated in German) and "Elohim." In English, we spell it "Yahweh." This was a personal name, and Elohim was just the generic word for god(s). As noted above, instead of spelling out the Name, we will use one of the other names, or THE NAME, or HaShem.

I would like to leave for later (section 7.4) the detective work by which these strands in the text were first dissected. That story belongs to the nineteenth century and the threshold of the modern world. It is enough here to look at the different theologies of the several editors of what we know as the Pentateuch, the first five books of the Bible, the Torah. Let me take them two at a time. The first are J and E near the start of the monarchy. Then the history of the monarchy needs to be told. Toward the end of the monarchy, an end looming ominously in sight, we can meet the Deuteronomist (the "D" of JEDP) and then after the monarchy is wiped out, "P," the Priestly editor, who presumably puts it all together.

J writes (or collects and edits) at around the time of Solomon, maybe later, but not by much. The J texts in the Pentateuch may or may not be the beginning of a story that went on to the Succession Narrative in 1 and 2 Samuel, one document from the same hand and composition. That is disputed. But J and the Succession Narrative were written at about the same time.

Looking at what J contributed to Genesis, one passage that stands out is the covenant with Abraham in Genesis 12. God gets Abraham out of bed and says, "You see all those stars? You're gonna have more children than there are stars up there." God then tells him to leave Mesopotamia where he grew up, and go to a land to be disclosed along the way. It is not, when you think about it, a reassuring proposition. We tend to read it knowing how it will turn out. But Abraham was seventy-five years old, and the whole idea sounds somewhat harebrained.

When Sarah found out about it, she laughed. Really, she did. And so her only son, born late in her life, was called Isaac, or Yitzhak, in Hebrew, Son of Laughter, or something like that. The first covenant began with a joke.

Look at what God actually says: The promises to Abraham are quite striking (he appears as Abram here, he has not been renamed yet):

> And the LORD spoke to Abram: "Go forth from your land, from your kindred and from your father's house to the land which I will show you; Thus I will make you a great people and bless you, and I will make your name great, so that you will effect blessing. I will bless those who bless you: but whoever despises you, him will I curse. So, then, all the families of the earth can gain a blessing in you. And Abram went, as the LORD had told him, and Lot went with him.

The idea is that Abraham is supposed to bring blessing to everybody he meets. But he is a klutz. He goes down to Egypt, and passes his wife off as his sister, so that Pharaoh won't kill Abraham when he wants to have an affair with his wife. Pharaoh finds out and protests, and then gets a blessing, for treating Abraham well. And so it goes; the rest of the Abraham stories are all about blessings for other people, and as he gets the hang of it, Abraham even tries to help.

How would this go over in the time of Solomon? Well, Solomon was supposed to be a blessing for all his subjects. He was not. But the texts are fairly clear, even if discreet, and they are a standard by which Solomon could diplomatically be judged. However J conceived his story, it was more than just a political reproach for a despot, phrased carefully lest its author come to a bad end. He had to hold up a history so that nothing explicit was said about Solomon, but those who could understand the history would get the message. That history inevitably raised questions, questions about how it all began. And so the beginning had to be pushed back, to Abraham, and then to well before Abraham. Along the way, more business gets taken care of than just the good example of Abraham alongside the unstated bad example of Solomon.

In the first place, J wants to set things up so that the monarchy really does get legitimated. That means he has to account for the various tribes, how they came together, and how they came into the promised land. That means some real pluralism, for they were a diverse lot. J makes it seem like they were all children of one patriarch, Abraham. They had many gods. J turns the names of all their gods into names of one God who unites them and promised the Land of Israel for them. All of this is business that gets taken care of as the story moves along.

There is one theme that might not be noticed today, because of the medical security against disease and infant death that we enjoy. God promises Abraham lots of children. And Abraham only sees one—one legitimate child, Isaac, son of Sarah. Ishmael, the son of Hagar the maidservant, gets written out of the story. Almost everybody else comes from Isaac, and even then the numbers don't start until Isaac's grandchildren, the children of Jacob. We take the survival of children for granted. We are afraid of overpopulation (though that is changing). They were afraid of barrenness. At least the patriarchs (and their wives) were; the big-city culture in Mesopotamia may well have been more afraid of overpopulation. That, too, may surprise us.

But there is a message in this concern about children. Human life is good, and so it is a good thing to bring children into the world. When J starts the whole story, he does it in the Garden of Eden. (The beginning of Genesis, up to chapter 2, verse 4, is from a later editor. We shall come to it in time.) For J, things just sort of get started, without all the lofty cosmology of chapter 1.

There had as yet been no rain. The scene is set, in upper Mesopotamia, and rain comes, and with it fertility. And hints of the flood that is later to come, though for now, the waters are well-behaved. Human beings get created, a man and a woman. They are set in a walled garden, given all they could want, told they can eat anything except the fruit of the tree of knowledge of good and evil. In other words, they are not to go defining differences between good and evil in life. It's *all* good. But they do taste, to see what life is like when you divide it into good and evil. And they do define some things to be evil instead of good. Life ever since has been one complaint after another.

J, or the editor who produced J, was among the most generous and open-hearted theologians history has known. His vision of human life was simple enough. Life is good, life is a gift, and the only thing you can do wrong is to reject parts of it as evil. Later theologians all pick up these themes. When the Priestly editor adds chapter 1 to Genesis, he makes God declare seven times that the created world is good. History was built in, or crept in, like a cat insinuating itself between your arms and the keyboard while it thinks you are not looking. History, as we shall see, was crucial, and the instincts of the J document get a lot of development later on.

3.4 E

There is another layer of stories, almost as old as J, often hard to separate from J with any confidence. It is known as "E," because it uses the name "Elohim" for God where J does not. E also probably wrote in the North, dominated by the tribe of Ephraim, where J wrote for Judah in the south. How to separate these texts we save for the story of the nineteenth century, when scholars first deciphered the sources and editing with confidence. For now, we need the theology and the social circumstances of E.

E is only fragments. If there was an original E document, not all of it got into the Bible. And there are traces; some E texts seem to refer to other E texts that are no longer in the Bible. So it is sometimes harder to put together E's theology. Nevertheless, there are contrasts enough with J before him and D and P after him.

E has things on his mind that do not appear in J. Dreams, more developed speeches, the Word of God, and last but not least, temptations. Temptation is the problem his texts addressed. The remedy is the Fear of the Lord: for those who fear the Lord are faithful to the Lord.

Fear is a somewhat strange word in this context. I am told that it is the same as the word for ordinary fright before danger, or for fear of an enemy who is stronger, hostile, and dangerous. For in that kind of fear, you do not like the person you fear. But more than that is involved. When I first taught "JEDP and all that," the idea that the first part of the Bible was written by four *human* editors, and not dictated to scribes by God, students sometimes would be hesitant or take fright. This is natural, for you are left apparently bereft of your old promises of security. In the old explanations, the tradition as it was received from the nineteenth century, God dictated every word, and that's how we know it is true, how we know it is reliable. Since we have a guarantee, we can trust the Bible. Supposedly. (That old tradition neglected to tell us how we could *know* the text came from God, but people usually didn't inquire into such things. A guarantee was a good thing, if you could get one; better not to ask questions that might make it evaporate.)

Then students get the hang of it. They begin to hear the message of J and E, and it is a message of grace, a message of permission to live. If J is a message of sunny goodness of life, E repeats the theme, with some variations. See what happens when Joseph's brothers come to him in the end of Genesis, afraid that he will take vengeance on them for selling him into slavery in Egypt. (After all, he is now the Grand Vizier, second only to Pharaoh himself, with effectively absolute power over all Egypt, themselves included.) As I say, they expect vengeance. That is not what happens. "Joseph answered them, 'Do not be afraid; is it for me to put myself in God's place? The evil you planned to do me has by God's design been turned to good, that he might bring about, as indeed he has, the deliverance of a numerous people. So you need not be afraid; I myself will provide for you and your dependents.' " (Gen. 50.19-21, Jerusalem Bible)

There are several themes here. Evil is converted into good—we will see that idea again and again. And fear should be fear of the right kind, fear of God that is also trust of God—but not fear of life, nor fear of evil. As I say, students get the hang of it when they see the Pentateuch taken apart into pieces, and then see the pieces located in real history, and a theology to go with each period in history.

It is more than a little like the joke about what happened when some Israeli archaeologists dug up Jesus' bones. They were cautious about going public with the news; after all, it looked as if the world's largest religion might have to go out of business, and they didn't want to get into trouble for being the bearers of the bad news. So they figured they had better tell the Pope first, and let him break the unhappy news to the Christian faithful. They told the Pope. And the Pope thought he had better tell the theologians before going public with the bad news, and maybe the theologians could help him with the sad task. So as he worked his way through his Rolodex sitting in Rome, he eventually came to one particularly crusty old Protestant north of the Alps, a theologian noted for his skepticism, for how little he would believe as historical. The Pope dreaded the call. But he told the story, as he had to the other theologians. There was a long silence at the north end of the phone. Finally, in tones of hushed awe, "Aach, so! Den he really did livf!"

Learning the real history of the Bible is like learning to ride a bicycle, at the stage where you first go without training wheels. The "literal" interpretation of the Bible functions like the training wheels. You can't fall over, but you also can't go very fast. Without training wheels you are precarious, you really *can* fall over, and at high speed, you may bruise your hands or knees. But then you realize that even at moderate speeds, you really do have enough control over the bike so that you can go someplace. And you never go back to training wheels. To appreciate what gets called "critical history" is to read the Bible without training wheels.

It is like that. When you see the roots of the Bible in real history, when you see the lives of men and women in faith in that far past, when you see that the same history you expect for secular questions shows you a solid history in the Bible, when you see all that, you would never go back to the quasi-magical theories of divine inspiration that we inherited from the nineteenth century. Theories of divine dictation look very fictional. But the Bible is real.

When students catch on, their initial fright turns to relish, and they come back for more. Thus does the fear of the Lord turn people on.

3.5 Elijah and Elisha

E probably wrote in the North, and knows traditions from the Northern kingdom. In the time between Elijah and Hosea, and from the point of view of the E writer (and later, D, even more so), Israel did indeed face temptations aplenty—first and last, the temptation to embrace the Baals and the Ashtartes, the Canaanite religion. Hans Walter Wolff and Walter Brueggemann (whose book makes an excellent guide to the theologies of the Pentateuch) profess themselves unable to locate E any more closely than that. There are not enough clues. But it was an interesting time, as the Elijah and Elisha stories tell us.

For here we see religious conflict at the heart of Israelite society. Before, in the time of David and Solomon, or of the Judges, conflicts were with Canaanites or Philistines, and relations with the Baals and Ashtartes (and their worshipers) were occasionally civil, perhaps even cordial. In fact, more than just cordial. Often the same people worshiped HaShem and the Baals and Ashtartes alike. Solomon accommodated the gods and goddesses of his foreign wives, and so far as the surviving texts tell us, this did not cause a problem. In the time of Ahab and Jezebel, it caused problems. We see violence aplenty—Jezebel slaughters the prophets of HaShem by the sword, and Elijah slaughters her minions by a word in return. Elijah summons the prophets of Baal to the mountain top and invites them to call on Baal to light their sacrifice (no matches allowed!). They dance, they gash themselves in sacred ecstasy, but there is no fire. Then Elijah soaks his sacrifice in water, calls on the Lord, and voilà: It is consumed in fire! An awesome story, thrilling special effects. There was no love lost between the Baal-folk and the no-other-gods party. We see along the way that Ahab and Jezebel are singularly despotic, unjust to their subjects, a theme that appeared earlier with Solomon and Rehoboam. And so the idea of justice appears explicitly as it has not before. It is an issue *within* Israelite society, and especially an issue for *Israelite* rulers, not foreign rulers.

How did we get here?

A lot has happened, and it is possible to draw some of it together. The memories of the Exodus are at work, they have shaped Israelite religion. It may be that only a small part of the later population of Israel ever came out of Egypt. Unlike the monarchy, the Exodus is untraceable for the historian. There is not enough surviving evidence. But whoever the people were who came out of Egypt, the memories that they brought with them grew in the telling and in the life of Israel and came to shape all of it later on.

In *The Waters of Naturalism*, there were seven lessons in the Exodus. Most of them are apparent at this point. In all probability, they were really seen and appreciated only in hindsight. History is often that way. We say that George Washington was the "father of his country," but during the events of the Revolution, that was not at all clear. People usually don't know what they are doing in history. Only later generations can see. The rabbis, at least, knew this; for in the Talmud, Moses gets to watch rabbi Akiba in his classroom, and Moses is dumbfounded that Akiba found such teaching in his Torah, the Torah that was given to him on Mt. Sinai.

But the memories of the Exodus were like memories of crossing a watershed. Some watersheds are dramatic, like crossing the knife-edge ridge of a hogback. Others are gentle and imperceptible, like central Wyoming, where the Continental Divide is quite flat. You would not know you were crossing it. The Exodus, whenever it happened, was just a movement of peoples out of Egypt. Migrant workers came, migrant workers left. Mostly nobody noticed, nobody cared. But these people (or their children) remembered, and they remembered their leaving somewhat strangely. It is not the Special Effects that I am interested in—though they served to remind people that something special was happening. It was the way these people fitted the events into their own life-story that was different.

As we saw in *Waters*, Moses led them out of nature and into history. (At least the Moses of memory did this, whatever may be conjectured about the Moses of fact.) With a sense of history, it was possible for them to stick together. In the order of nature, they would have been just a diverse lot of tribes, soon at each other's throats. But in the openness of history, they could become allies and then one people, not natural enemies.

We can see the lessons of the Exodus at work in the life of Israel during the time of the Kings and prophets. Already, the king is not divine, the king is not above criticism. The prophets criticize—and they do so on the basis of the remembered stories of the Exodus. We were rescued, we were saved, we were brought into this land, it was given to us, and so you should be grateful, you the King should treat us your subjects with generosity and justice. To receive a great gift and then not to pass it on would be gross ingratitude. Gratitude was at the heart of these memories, and at the heart of the way of life that grew out of them.

The Israelites were a diverse lot. No merely natural account of their coming together could hold them together, although the genealogy as sons of Jacob in some ways works like a naturalistic account. But they were joined by many foreigners, even on the strictest reading of the genealogy. The sacred in nature loses its power at this point. These people had a somewhat strange sense of what counts in life. We would say it was essentially historical, because history is open in ways that nature is not. Nature doesn't give you choices, history does, but with choice comes responsibility. In history, you have to take responsibility for your life. There is no responsibility in nature, and so none of the anxiety that comes with responsibility. These people did not do *philosophy* of history, not even remotely. But they did develop a sense of their own history, of where they had come from, and of how they had come into the Promised Land.

For this project to work, they needed some standards of acceptable behavior, and they needed to remember their origins in history. All that is present now: for the first parts of the Law in Exodus come from J and E, and the sense of history is implicit in the epics that J and E wrote. These themes will be filled out as we move forward, but they are present already at this stage.

These peoples came together from many places. The God who was to hold them together had to combine the features of all the gods that these people brought with them on their way into Israel. And so he did. The names survive—but they have all become names for the one God. El, El Elyon, El Shaddai, El Olam, El Bethel, and so on. "El" is a kind of generic name for god(s), and the El of a place was the local deity of that place. They were all combined into one, they all became names for one. The Baals were included at the start, though they have been removed from the records and only traces remain. This may be a result of the fighting between pluralists (the Baal-folk) and anti-pluralists (to become the no-other-gods party) in the time of Elijah and after. But Gideon is also named Jerub-baal, and Psalm 29 is originally a hymn to Baal the storm god. What the editors have done is craft a story in which THE NAME does not reveal his name until late in the story, in the encounter with Moses in Exodus. Thus we have different peoples, different patriarchs who know THE NAME under other names. And so many peoples came together, bringing many gods with them.

The fifth lesson that we found in *Waters* has only its roots in the time of the monarchy. It didn't blossom until the Hellenistic period. This is the lesson that says God comes to you to bless a good world, rather than to get you out of an evil world. Much of the Hellenistic world, faced with its own pains, will seek escape from this world to a transcendence that is supposedly better. Then covenanters will realize how important it is to welcome transcendence into this world, where it can do some good. But even the seeds of this lesson are clearly present in the earlier texts. For the world is declared to be good, and the troubles in life come from calling evil parts of a life that are good. This is the whole point of J's account of eating the apple in the Garden of Eden. Why was one tree forbidden? Because its fruit enables you to define differences between good and evil in life. We shall see this lesson deepened greatly after the Exile, to which we come momentarily.

Return to the multiple names of God. This is the face of a real pluralism, and it is easily missed or ignored in reading the texts. It was generous and accommodating to a fault. It was open to all. At early stages, the LORD even had a wife. There is a picture of her. It is a faint tracing of an ink drawing on a potsherd, "To Jahweh and His Asherah," little more than graffiti, crude drawings that would be at home in grade-school art today. The pot with this picture on it was found at Kuntillet 'Ajrud, a site on the edge of the desert from late in the ninth century BCE or early in the eighth. The graffito of the Deity and Wife is reproduced in a slide collection and its accompanying guide book (McCarter, 1996; p. 107).

This is just the period we are interested in, the middle of the monarchy. It was a time of relative prosperity and security for the two kingdoms, Israel and Judah. They were left alone by the great empires to the north-east and south-west, in Mesopotamia and Egypt. (Neither was strong enough to interfere, for a few centuries.) There were records, the Annals of the Kings of Israel, the Annals of the Kings of Judah. They have been lost, but they are cited often in the biblical books of Kings.

If it was a time of prosperity, it was also a time of religious conflict. As often happens, people could not agree on how to conduct a covenant. What goes for "religion" as we know it goes for politics as well, for they were the same thing in those days. They were given a stage on which to play out their lives and freedom to do so. And so they thought about it all—what they were doing, how one should live, how a covenant community should order its life together.

That might sound like it was all a solemn and pious deliberation. It was not. As often as not, they squabbled among themselves. Sometimes the quarrels were later forgotten, sometimes there was lasting bitterness. Mostly it was gluttony, orgies, petty abuses of power and misrule. But that is enough to make people think, and think they did.

And they wrote; how they wrote. For this is the time of the first prophets. The writing that survives is not large in volume. You could miss the minor prophets entirely in the Bible if you turn pages too fast. But the writing is eloquent, it cries from the heart. Usually poetry, promises of help, comfort in misery, threats of retribution, shame for the faithless, encouragement for the remnant. Now the prophets were in some ways like shamans of other societies, and the prophet had taken over the functions of a shaman, but with a difference.

Prophets raved, just like shamans. Prophets could hear and see the invisible where ordinary people could not. People came to a shaman when they wanted answers, and the prophets were not much different in *that* respect. But sometimes the prophet came to the people, or to the king, unasked. And a shaman would tell you what nature holds for your life. Here, the prophets were different. For it was not something merely invisible in nature that they spoke for, but something transcendent, and more importantly, something that shows itself in history, not nature. In nature, things are orderly, and people came to a shaman when they wanted to know how to fit into the order of nature, or how to restore the order of nature. Disorder was evil. Prophets called people back to history, to gratitude for their lot in history, to a sense of responsibility for their actions. In history, disorder is not evil, disorder is just a fact of life. But without the order of nature, you are not entirely in control, and so history can be terrifying.

3.6 D, Deuteronomy, Disaster

History was terrifying indeed as the end of the monarchy approached. Life had been good to these people in the centuries before. They even concocted a covenant in which ultimate reality, the dim unknown transcendent that is behind history, had promised them a monarchy that would last forever. But reality set in soon enough. For the kingdom of David and Solomon was possible in the tenth and ninth centuries BCE only because Assyria to the northeast and Egypt to the southwest were weak and unable to interfere. That changed. Assyria came back on the horizon during the years of conflict about Israelite religion, conflicts about how to live rightly, how to rule justly, and how to worship—or more to the point, *which* gods to worship. The prophets could see disaster coming, as it did for little Israel in 722 BCE, and a century and a half later for littler Judah. Actually, everybody could see disaster coming. Perhaps some were in denial, but all understood the possibility. They didn't like it. What people could not hear at all was the idea that some good might come out of the disaster. But the prophets had the audacity to claim that in the coming doom was Israel's true hope.

How on earth could the prophets think such a thing?! It is fairly easy to jump to the conclusion that anything bad must be a punishment. That was the simple explanation, before, during, and after the disaster. But things were not so simple, and the disaster was not just a punishment. For in history lies the possibility of relationship, relationship with a mystery that lies beyond any particular actor in history. And relationships are forged and tested and deepened most strongly when things are difficult: Easy come, easy go, but a friend in need is a friend indeed.

We have seen already, in *Unwelcome Good News*, the question *why* one should embrace the pains of life as blessing-bearing, opportunity-offering, freedom-bringing. In the end (or better, in the beginning), the short answer and the best answer is that's just The Way Things Are. One gets to know how things are in history, in the course of working through life. In responsibility, openness, and freedom you come up face to face with—with what? With yourself, with a radical question, do you want to affirm life as it is, here and now, when it's hard? The editors who wrote Deuteronomy (D, our next contribution to the Bible) never put the question that way. They were not theoreticians, much less existentialist philosophers. For them, it was enough to forbid visible images of the ultimate reality, pictures and statues. "No images" was a very concrete and graphic way of representing what we would call transcendence. The combination of no images plus prayers to the deity was highly paradoxical. It could be a little terrifying, like a sort of High-Church Atheism.

But the voices of complaint (that's what the prophets were, after all) had grubby everyday affairs on their minds. Their message was one of attention to history, and gratitude for history, gratitude for the accidents that had given them the Land that was theirs. If so, then maybe it would help to retell that history, and maybe it would help to spell out how you're supposed to live because of it. In other words, let's have (1) The Story, and (2) a Law, so we can know what to do and not do, and know why.

And so someone put together a new Law, a "Second Law," for that's what "Deutero-nomy" means. At least some of the legal texts in Exodus are probably older than Deuteronomy, but it's hard to tell what circulation or status they had during the late years of the monarchy. How all this came to pass takes a little telling.

The last few kings of Judah stand out. In 733 BCE, Tiglath-Pileser, the King of Assyria, humbled Israel, and destroyed it permanently in 722. King Ahaz of Judah submitted voluntarily and payed tribute. Judah outlasted the Assyrians. (Remember limitation, from *Unwelcome Good News*?) Within a few years of 725, plus or minus, Ahaz died and his son Hezekiah became king of Judah. Hezekiah was no friend of his Assyrian masters, and participated in such insubordination as he could get away with.

The prophet Isaiah was Hezekiah's contemporary. This was the first Isaiah. It comes as a surprise that there was more than one Isaiah, but chapter 40 ("Comfort, comfort my people . . .") comes from a later period and a later hand. We come to it in a moment. Evidently prophets had students (Elisha was Elijah's student, after all), and the sayings of the teacher were treasured—and sometimes continued—by the students. Memory of what the master had said could become quite creative. Creative enough, indeed, to remember what the master *would* have said, were he alive today. Discerning readers can see how the texts were put together.

The frontier kingdoms in the southwest of the Assyrian empire often withheld taxes or engaged in open revolt. Judah, Ashdod and Gaza on the seacoast, Ammon and Moab and Edom in the desert; they all tried to play off Egypt against Assyria. Hezekiah's opportunity came when the Assyrians were distracted and weakened, and he stopped the tribute. Now part of the duty of a vassal king was to host the gods of the overlord. And so images of the Assyrian gods and goddesses were living in the Temple in Jerusalem. It was these that Hezekiah trashed at the same time as he stopped paying taxes.

As we have already seen, people couldn't agree about whether it was acceptable to worship the whole crowd of the gods, instead of just the One God, HaShem. Never mind the diplomatic issues, the *realpolitik*. Was it *right*? Should we interpret the first commandment literally? No other gods? Obviously the no-other-gods party rejoiced when Hezekiah threw out the foreign idols.

As often happens, a change of administration is also a change of party. It was that way with Manasseh, Hezekiah's son. Manasseh ruled for 50 years or so. Manasseh was a supremely successful diplomat and politician. Part of his diplomatic success came from accommodating images of the gods and goddesses of the nations he was allied with, and of the empire he was subject to. If you and I make an alliance, we trade images of each other's gods, so that my gods can keep an eye on you, and your gods can keep an eye on me. And I can sweet-talk your gods face-to-face, as I hope you will do for mine. Manasseh did all this. Manasseh was execrated by the no-other-gods party. They loathed him and his memory. Manasseh had reversed Hezekiah's policy completely, for Hezekiah was "cruising for a bruising," and Manasseh knew how to avoid trouble. Whatever was left of Hezekiah's reforms was hidden during Manasseh's reign. Hidden and then forgotten. As things played out later, the historians were of Hezekiah's party, the no-other-gods party. Manasseh's successes are mostly passed over in silence in the Bible, because the editors were embarrassed that such an evil king could have such good results.

When Josiah came to the throne, the no-other-gods party was back in power. Josiah set about a religious reform that was much more radical than anything Hezekiah had attempted. He abolished ritual and sacrifice at every altar outside of Jerusalem, thereby making it possible to keep control over what ritual remained, strictly enforcing the program of the no-other-gods party.

At some point during Josiah's reign, the priests in the Temple found a scroll of legal material. It may have been left by priests during

Hezekiah's reign, but that is just speculation. It was not entirely welcome, because the people were not "in compliance" with its rules, as gum-shoes would say today. This is the text we know as Deuteronomy, or at least as the heart of the book of Deuteronomy. Josiah called a big town-meeting in Jerusalem, and got the people to agree to keep this new law. Scholars call such a meeting a covenant renewal ceremony, the rite by which the people renew their commitment to a covenant. It is hard to say how old the tradition of a covenant ratification ceremony was, but evidently it was already considered traditional then. There is one in the end of Joshua, for example.

Josiah's opportunity did not last long. The Assyrian empire was crumbling, because the Babylonians had not only revolted in the south of Mesopotamia, but were well on their way to replacing the Assyrians with a new and stronger empire. Egypt was inclined to keep the old and familiar enemy rather than face one new and more dangerous. Josiah was allied with the Babylonians, hoping to get rid of his old enemy for good. In the scrap with the Egyptians that followed, Josiah was killed, and soon the Babylonians, erstwhile friends, were the new overlords in Syria-Palestine. Josiah's heirs made the mistake of resisting them, and soon Judah was destroyed. In 598 BCE, the Babylonians deported most of the ruling class from Jerusalem to Babylon. In 586 BCE, they finished the job after Judah revolted again. Jerusalem was burned to the ground. The Temple was destroyed on the ninth of Ab, the month in the Hebrew calendar that usually falls in August. In a coincidence, when the Second Temple was destroyed by the Romans in 70 CE, it was once again the ninth of Ab. The date is remembered in the Synagogue to this day. It would not hurt the Church to remember it as well. Christian readers, who usually treat places of worship as disposable, are not used to the high value that the Temple held in Israelite religion.

Chapter 4

Pulling It All Together

4.1 Comfort, Comfort, My People

Everybody knows the opening to Handel's *Messiah*, "Comfort ye, comfort ye, my people," but the history behind that tender plaintive tenor's song is not as well known. The first few verses of Isaiah chapter 40 announce hope in time of disaster, a promise of return to the Land of Israel after a few brief decades of exile. Make straight in the desert a highway for our God: in other words, the highway from Baghdad to Tel Aviv, today; then, from Babylon to the ruins of Jerusalem. Today, the road is truly straight, across the desert of Iraq and Jordan. Modern engineers can indeed "exalt" every valley, and make low hills and mountains. Driving the interstate highway through the mountains (e.g. the Pennsylvania Turnpike through the Alleghenies) shows you what the second Isaiah could only imagine. Quite some imagination: for he was promising what was then impossible. But the remembered tradition of the escape from Egypt was about to be repeated, and it had special effects (the parting of the sea), and so this second Exodus should have equally spectacular promises as well.

The promise was unbelievable enough. For the kingdom of Israel had disappeared utterly, absorbed into the other peoples of upper

Mesopotamia by the Assyrians. The idea that Judah should fare any better was not to be expected. But the Babylonians were more tolerant than the Assyrians. In any case, they lasted only a scant forty years after the destruction of the Temple, for the Persians conquered and replaced them around 540 BCE. The Persian policy was very generous by the standards of those days: conquered peoples were not to be deported, and those that had been were allowed to return.

Second Isaiah sees all this as the hand of the Lord, and in a sense it was. Unbelievable as it was, Isaiah's promise came true. In Handel, the theme builds up from a single thin, tremulous and hesitant voice to a full chorus in a grand crescendo. But Handel is just following the text. For the message of the second Isaiah was not just one of hope, not just a hard to believe one-in-a-million chance, something that will go away if you blink your eyes. It was much grander, much more unbelievable than that. For Isaiah has it that it was all planned. El Jefe, the Boss, the God of the patriarchs and the Exodus, is very much in charge, directing events with a sure hand, not to be shaken. To be sure, behind the scenes, not visible to human eye, not to be put to the test by untrusting human hearts. But very much in charge.

Isaiah, Jeremiah, and Ezekiel, the three "major" prophets, their students and editors, were all of the no-other-gods party. Jeremiah (and the first Isaiah, approximately chapters 1-39) wrote before the disaster was consummated, and wrote in hope for an uncertain future. Ezekiel and the second Isaiah wrote when the return was visible, in hope for a future about to happen. Ezekiel travels back and forth from the exiles in Babylon to the recent past in Jerusalem. Isaiah just sings.

They have two themes, each presented in his own way. Ezekiel is the more graphic of the two; Isaiah has words to make your ears burn—or your heart warm. Ezekiel is appalled by the the idols that were in the Temple in Jerusalem side-by-side with the throne of HaShem. (See ch. 8, esp. vv. 9–10.) Isaiah has only scorn and satire for such idols. (Check out ch. 44.9–20, about the man who burns half a log to cook his food, and makes a statue out of the other half, a statue he then bows down to and asks to bestow prosperity on him and his wife and children.) Ezekiel shows us the most that we can see of the deity: a light shining out of a cloud, escorted by heralds on wheels. ("Ezekiel saw the wheel!", ch. 1) The point of the wheels, and they are set on universal bearings, is that they can roll in any direction. The mechanical engineering details are left out. And these heralds levitate. This God can travel, this God has wheels, it (and its heralds) can go *anywhere*.

Ezekiel shows us the eye-candy, spectacular visions, no small feat given only words to work with. To be sure, the visions are discreet: The deity we are not allowed to see, because human eye and human mind are not capable of seeing. But we do see the light.

Isaiah's God is presented to us not in graphic images but in what he does. He is greater than the Persian conquerors; in fact, he has appointed the Persian Cyrus to be the one to "set things right," to restore the Lord's chosen people to their homeland. But restoration is for more than that; they are to resume their relationship with the deity that is invisible in and behind history. Together, they walk through history.

Isaiah's God is grand. He travels, as Ezekiel told us. He is everywhere, not just the local god-franchise for this or that valley or tribe and clan. He is sovereign.

Now you might think this means he is "all-powerful," or "omnipotent," or some such modern word meaning "able to do anything, caprice and whimsy without restraint." That is not *quite* what Isaiah had in mind. It is more like this: despite whatever mishaps may befall the people faithful to him, he will be faithful to them, he will take care of them, even in the disasters of history.

Or, if you want the same thing without mention of the deity (for our present age, when the idea of "God" is so preposterous to so many), it was a faith that no matter what happened, even in the worst disasters history could deal them, the people of Israel would ultimately find blessing. That's what Isra-el means: the people that struggles with

God. They do not exactly win, in the sense of triumphing over ultimate reality, but they do gain a blessing. That faith was to be tested many times in the centuries that followed, not least in our own time, in the Shoah, the Destruction of the European Jews in the twentieth century.

Look at what Isaiah does. He has only derision for the other gods. Where there was disagreement during the years of the monarchy, about whether one should worship the whole host of Heaven, or only the one Lord, the no-other-gods party has triumphed here. The names of many of the other gods are preserved as we noticed briefly, preserved as synonyms for "Jahweh." In some places, even "Baal" is included. But especially "El," "Elohim," and the colloquial "Adonai," meaning El Jefe, The Boss.

Isaiah sees all the essential parts of the problem. He doesn't (to the best of my limited knowledge) edit the texts in the Pentateuch or the history that follows, the texts in which the names of God and all the histories are combined into the history of one God. But he does see that if this deity is really to be sovereign, and if this deity is to pull off the insane project of being the patron of an insignificant people tossed among the great powers at the center of the known world, then this deity is going to have to deal with weakness, this deity is going to have to deal with suffering. For he allows suffering enough for his supposedly chosen people. There is the problem: power in weakness, power for weakness.

It is in the four Servant Songs, Isaiah 42.1-9, 49.1-6, 50.4-9, and 52.13-53.12, that we see the call of Jacob, the Servant of the Lord, the one who struggles, who suffers, who suffers for others, who is not conspicuous or "powerful." This is the one whose suffering is to bring justice?!

It is the fourth Servant Song that is best known, again from Handel's Messiah: "Surely he hath borne our griefs, and carried our sorrows, he was wounded for our transgressions," and so on. We know these verses because in yet another great disaster five hundred years later, all of Judaism was disrupted, much of it was destroyed, and one of the two surviving major parties used these texts in Isaiah to make sense of its life. We haven't gotten that far yet. This comes from the Exile, it is just about the Jewish people and their struggles. No wonder Jacob gets renamed Israel.

Look at what Isaiah says.

> Though you do not know me, I arm you
> that men may know from the rising of the sun
> to the setting of the sun
> that, apart from me, all is nothing.
>
> I am the LORD, unrivalled,
> I form the light and create the dark.
>
> I make good fortune and create calamity,
> it is I, the LORD, who do all this.
> . . .
> Can it argue with the man who fashioned it,
> one vessel among earthen vessels?
> Does the clay say to its fashioner,
> 'What are you making?'
> does the thing shaped say, 'You have no skill'?
> . . .
> I it was who made the earth,
> and created man who is on it.

It stands at the origin of the world, and of man in the world. The good and the evil alike come from this ultimate reality. It brings good *in* the evil. That is Isaiah's solution to Israel's otherwise intractable problem.

This deity is not all-powerful in the way we would call a super-human dictator all-powerful, able to do anything he wants, subject to no limitation, logical or illogical. But it is The Way Things Are, and with it there is in the end no bargaining, though one may struggle with it and still be faithful to it. When you start talking to ultimate reality, when you start talking to The Way Things Are, then, of course, you are in some danger (*Unwelcome Good News*, ch. 5). Is it really all-powerful like a human despot? That mistake was made early and often by Christians in the seventeenth century, and it still is in the present. It is that mistake that Monty Python lampooned in a skit in *The Meaning of Life*. ("Oooh you are so big ... So absolutely huge ... Gosh, we're all really impressed down here I can tell you.") How a mighty theology has fallen.

Look at Psalm 111, to get some idea of how this theology started out. Some think this Psalm comes from later than the Exile, and so from later than the second Isaiah. It is not bad as a summary of the project of deutero-Isaiah. You can see where Monty Python got their material; the Psalm has it that "Great are the deeds of the Lord, . . . His work is full of majesty and splendor." But there is more than that here. You might not notice, but there is a capsule summary of the history in this short Psalm, for he "sent redemption to his people," and as a consequence, "commanded his covenant forever." There is enough about the good that this deity has showered on his people, but there is also more than you might think about remembering and gratitude.

This is trust that no matter what happens, no matter how bad it gets, life is good, life is a blessing. We shall see how it unfolds. Deutero-Isaiah offered a second Exodus, but it was more than that: it was a radicalizing of the Exodus experience.

4.2 The Way of Historical Religion

These people were not philosophers, they were not speculative theorists, and they certainly did not do metaphysics. All that comes later. But they did think about what it takes to do a religion this way, what it takes to affirm human life in history. They knew they didn't like the many gods of their neighbors, and they had to figure out how to avoid what they didn't like, and figure out what they wanted to do instead.

Actually, some people in Israel did very much like what their neighbors were doing; the neighbors' gods were guests in the Temple in Jerusalem until the time of the Exile. And the practice of getting help to find out what was going to happen in the future was universal. If the consultant was one of your own, he was a prophet; if he worked for some other gods, he (or she) was a fortune-teller, a witch, or in modern terms, a shaman. The difference was easily fudged.

How do you do a religion in history? How do you make history central in your life? They certainly wanted to keep one thing—the world-affirming part of the nature religions they had grown up with. Actually, they kept a lot more, but they transformed virtually everything. Here is a clue. You can see it in the rituals of thanksgiving for the harvest festivals. Where normally you would expect the thanks to be directed to nature (we would say "*Mother* Nature"), the thanks are instead directed to a deity that is Lord of History, the one who brought these people out of Egypt. Clearly, the experience of whomever it was who came out of Egypt those many centuries before spread like a slow fire, to all the rest of the Israelites in the land of Canaan. Eventually it was as if burned into their consciousness.

You can begin with the Exodus from Egypt, or with the editors (some centuries later), who left us the story of the Exodus. Either way, something big changed, even though we often don't notice when we read the Bible.

When *they* began with "in the beginning . . . ," they actually made some real changes in the story. For the beginning of the world is no longer just a cosmogony, it has become a creation, and the difference matters. A cosmogony is just the coming-into-being of the cosmos. Creation is also a *blessing*. Seven times, in the first account in Genesis, the God pronounces the world and everything in it to be good. In the original versions, from the surrounding cultures, it is a contest between good and evil, and good wins—but just barely. Let me come to the actual text in the Bible in the next section, and here look only at how the world is changed in it. For here, creation is the beginning of history rather than the model for nature. Nature is orderly, and history is essentially disorderly. You have to have some disorder if there is to be freedom. We take it for granted that freedom is a good thing, but they did not. Disorder in the ancient world was bad, and the rituals of the world-affirming nature religions were all designed to restore the natural order of things—in the human world, the natural world, and in the cosmos. That's why an eclipse of the sun or the moon was so threatening, by the way; it was disorder in the worst way. When you come to the Israelites, they found earthquakes and volcanoes to be exhilarating. This was not entirely original. Psalm 29, an earthquake psalm most emphatic, was stolen from the Baal-worshippers at Ugarit. And in nature, the contest between order and disorder is a near thing. A good outcome is not at all obvious.

But when disorder is embraced as part of the good world that is to be affirmed, then you have to make some adjustments. You have choices you did not have before. You no longer can rely on nature to tell you what to do. You need some way for people to get along other than "just fit into nature naturally."

You would naturally feel alone and abandoned if nature and natural order no longer provide the sense of a home in the cosmos. And so these people turned the gods into a companion in history. Actually, they turned many gods into *one* companion, one that had the name of what was probably a local volcano and earthquake deity from the Sinai, but that is just conjecture. What follows is like a wedding, an engagement, a voluntary arrangement. It is not negotiated—the deity is powerful, after all, and cannot be coerced or manipulated—but it is still a voluntary commitment, as you will notice if you read carefully.

How true this was! For it took many centuries before the religion of Jahweh (that's the name of this volcano and earthquake deity) was able to melt the original gods into one, to transform the original nature religions into a religion of history. All this seems to be long in the past, for the editors who write after the return from Babylon. It looks to them as if this new religion was delivered whole many centuries before, and the people had been alternately faithful and unfaithful over the centuries since. In fact, the truth was probably much more like a gradual conversion of habits, a gradual morphing of nature religion into a historical religion.

But look how it seemed to them, in the eyes of yet later rabbis who looked back on it all. There is a midrash (a meditation, if you like) on the covenant at Sinai that appears in the beginning of the Great Midrash on Song of Songs. Each of the commandments of the Law (there are six hundred thirteen, not just ten) is addressed to each Israelite in turn.

> An angel carried the utterances [at Mount Sinai] from before the Holy One, blessed be He, each one in turn, and brought it to each of the Israelites and said to him, "Do you take upon yourself this commandment? So-and-so many rules are attached to it, so-and-so many penalties are attached to it, so-and-so many precautionary measures are attached to it, so many precepts and so many lenient and strict applications are attached to it." (Midrash Rabbah Song of Songs (Soncino, 1983), I.2,2, pp. 21–22.)

And each Israelite in turn answers Yes.

In another story, this one in the Bible, you can see the sense of loneliness that comes with leaving nature for history. Look at the job interview when Moses gets hired to bring the Israelites out of Egypt. We saw this in *Waters*, and saw Moses having a typical shaman's vision, when the voice from the burning bush tells Moses to do a very un-shamanly thing: go back to Egypt and lead his people out of nature, and into history.

What did Moses do? What would *you* do with a talking bush telling you to go home and take all your friends out into the desert? (Go camping without any electricity, without even any portable electronics, and *never come back*?) Moses says to the bush, of course, "Who *are* you?" "Who *ARE* you?" "Whom shall I say has sent me?"

And what the bush answers is not very comforting. It just says, "I shall be with you as who I am shall I be with you." Not entirely reassuring, not entirely grammatical. At least that is how John Courtney Murray made it, in his comments on Exodus 3.14. It usually comes out in translation as "I am who am," which doesn't help us much. Sometimes "I will be who I will be," which is a little better, but still none too clear. I shall be with you, you will not be abandoned or bereft, but you will not see me.

Moses went. The Israelites left Egypt, and with Egypt, left nature religion. Were they abandoned? *They* thought so. They complained. "Were there not graves enough in Egypt that you had to bring us out here in the desert to die?" Was there not disorder enough even in nature, that you had to bring us out here into history, to be *totally* confused? Starved, attacked, chased all over hellan'gone, and then eaten alive?

We know the story. They made it into the promised land, and centuries later, the writers and storytellers had to make sense of it all. The prophets reproached them with forgetting. But they did not forget. Perhaps only a few of the peoples who came into the Land of Israel actually came out of Egypt as migrant laborers (as we noticed in the beginning of chapter 3). But the memory of the Exodus spread from them like a computer virus and infected everybody. Soon it had taken over everything they did, it shaped their lives. The rest of our story in this book is to see how, and to see the consequences.

4.3 P

After the return from Babylon, we are at a time of taking-stock, a time when the writers sat down and asked themselves what had happened. If the Exodus was the watershed, the point of moving from nature into history, it was only a long time afterward that they realized what had happened to them. In section 3.5 I likened the Exodus to the crossing of the Continental Divide in central Wyoming. Look closer. We think of crossing the Continental Divide as being like Interstate

70 west of Denver, at Loveland Summit, which is quite dramatic and unmistakable. But Interstate 80 in south-central Wyoming crosses the Divide *twice*, and you wouldn't know you were crossing the Divide either time. (In between is the Great Divine Basin, which doesn't drain at all.) Later, when the streams flow west, you might suspect. But only when you have come down the pass through the Wasatch mountains into the Great Salt Lake valley and the Bonneville salt flats, only then can you look back and see that the mountain heights are to the *east* of you instead of ahead of you, to the west. Then you know how far you have come. The exiles returning from Babylon had a long way still to go, as the reader well knows. But the hardest parts were over, the defining moment was in the past.

So it is only natural that the Exodus events were pulled together much later than they actually happened. The Exodus was a tradition long before it was written up in the texts we have now. Quite a bit of writing comes from this period after the Babylonian Exile. A lot of the writing from this time was an attempt to salvage even older documents, many of which have perished. But what is surprising is that they didn't all perish. And the editors had stories of their own to tell. The stories that we have already seen, as J, E, and D, were combined with a fourth account of the tradition.

It is called the "Priestly" narrative, because it was put together by writers who show a particular interest in the Temple and things to do with it. This is the "P" in the name "JEDP" for the composition and editing of the first five books of the Bible. They are sometimes known as the Pentateuch (Greek for "five books"), or simply the Torah. For they were *the* teaching, and Torah just means teaching. That is, they became the central teaching for the people who had returned from exile and rebuilt Jerusalem and revived the covenant that had seemed to be gone for ever when Nebuchadnezzar burnt Jerusalem and the Temple.

When the exiles returned, they did rebuild the Temple, under Ezra and Nehemiah. This was the Second Temple, and it lasted (with a little remodeling) until the Romans destroyed it in 70 CE, some four or five hundred years. A temple requires priests, and the priests were the chief religious officers. They were the ones to hold the people together under Persian rule, the ones to give the people a sense of how to continue. This they did with a story of how it all came to be. The larger story actually has two parts, the first part being from the beginning of the world to the Exodus from Egypt (Genesis to Numbers), and the second part from the Exodus out of Egypt to the Babylonian Exile (Deuteronomy to 2 Kings). The second part of the story has a different flavor, and is not interested in ritual or the law; it is known as the Deuteronomic History, because it feels so much like Deuteronomy. It comes from a different editor (or editors) who are known simply as the Deuteronomic Historian, because the history starts in Deuteronomy and continues through the years of the monarchy. P cut the book of Deuteronomy out of the Deuteronomic History and left the rest of that history in the books of Joshua, Judges, Samuel and Kings.

P loved ritual, D was allergic to it. This is hardly surprising: P was the voice of the priests, after all, and their bread and butter was people who came to the Temple needing sacrifices. D was the historical voice of prophets, and they were often enough *against* ritual, because ritual covered up social and ethical abuses. But they (or their students) both worked at about the same time, and in a way, they worked together, for they were both of the no-other-gods party, and they had to figure out a way to continue after the Exile. This they did, with some compromises between them. (Pluralism is back, even here.)

The priestly narrative is about an earlier time, before the monarchy, from the beginning of the world to the entry into the Land of Israel. It is the matrix into which the earlier stories of J, E, and D are fitted. The last editor usually writes the first preface, and so it was with the Priestly editor. He contributes the creation story that begins in Genesis 1 and runs through Genesis 2.4.

4.4 Seven Lessons of the Exodus

In *Waters*, we saw seven lessons in the Exodus. They are not complicated.

(1) Human governments are to be held responsible for their actions. They are not divine, not to put themselves above criticism.

(2) This people was to be an open community of moral obligation; anyone could join, and so they were supposed to enjoy a certain pluralism.

(3) The nature gods lose their status, in part because they were clan gods (and so would divide people, not unite them), and in part because the focus shifts from nature to history. Actually, the nature gods get fused into one, the Lord of History.

(4) That Lord of History is manifest in history, but is also transcendent to history (and even more, transcendent to nature). That is, you can see his works, but you can't exactly see the God *himself*.

(5) The believer is to find God here in this world with us, because this world is good, rather than try to escape from this world to the God because this world is evil. In this lesson we were somewhat ahead of ourselves, for it does not really become an issue until a few centuries after the return from the Babylonian Exile, in the early centuries of the common era. We come to that soon enough. But the roots of even this lesson are there, as in Deuteronomy 30.11-13 strongly hints: the Law is not up in heaven, or across the sea, that you should have to go and find it, but closer to you than your heart. As with the Law, so with the God. And Genesis 1 seven times declares the world to be good.

(6) There has to be some concrete guide to how to do it all. In *Waters*, I said it was a behavioral standard, but it is more than that.

(7) Lastly, it is important to remember the history, to remember how all this came to be.

Let me expand some on (4) and (6). What might it mean for some reality that you can't see to show itself in history, and what might it mean to shape your life in a relationship to that reality? That reality can be named in many ways, doubtless, but one of my favorites is just the street-language that we saw in *Unwelcome Good News*, the exasperation of one who is tired of answering questions about why he does what he does. In the end, he just says, "Because that's The Way Things Are." But this is not an end, it is a beginning, for it is from this The Way Things Are that he starts to shape his life. The directions for the shaping are in the sixth lesson, and the focus of the shaping is in the fourth lesson. And it is not something that one man can do on his own; this is a group project.

So what are these people doing? Doing with their lives? They are wandering through history, often lost, always uncertain, yet wandering with that something, that presence in absence, that voice that spoke to Moses out of the burning bush. Lonely yet comforted. Tossed about yet confident. Bewildered yet with a sense of wherefrom and whereto. And with a sense of identity, a sense of being a people, a community, of having a life together.

4.5 From P to the First Century

The Priestly editors and their friends put things back together again under Persian rule. The story is in Ezra and Nehemiah. They rebuilt the Temple in Jerusalem, and the new temple is known today to scholars as the "Second Temple," to distinguish it from Solomon's Temple. It has given its name to the Judaism that lasted until the first century, when the Romans destroyed it in 70 CE. Second Temple Judaism was a time of flowering, a collecting and editing of texts, and a Judaism without the compromises with nature religions that so spooked the Deuteronomists.

The Persians ruled the Land of Israel until Alexander the Great came through, a little before 312 BCE. Alexander's heirs divided up his empire after him, and the Seleucids got Syria, the east, and the Land of Israel. The Ptolemies got Egypt, and made Alexandria their royal city. The Ptolemies were more tolerant than the Seleucids, and a

Jewish community grew up in Alexandria that lasted until well into the Common Era. The Seleucids wanted to impose Greek culture on all their subjects, to unify the empire. Second Temple Judaism was quite fierce in its opposition to any compromises with "idolatry," and most of the politically acceptable cults in Hellenistic society would qualify as idolatry. So the Jews of the period didn't get along with their neighbors. Where the Persians had been tolerant of subject peoples' religions, the Greek rulers in Syria were not.

Antiochus Epiphanes, the emperor we are interested in, decreed that all the Jews would have to quit circumcising their male children, eat pork in public, and other such things. They revolted. The story is in the books of Maccabees; they are in Catholic Bibles after Tobit, Judith and Esther, and before Job. In Protestant Bibles, they are in the Apocrypha. There are two of them, but they are not sequential, they are just two different versions of the same story. One is by the party that later became the Sadducees, and the name of God is not mentioned once in it. The other is by the party that became the Pharisees, and the story is, to put it gently, very pious. From the same time, by the way, come the books of Daniel and Esther, both thoroughly fictional, historical novels set in the time of the Persians three or four centuries earlier, but with enough of the fabulous (and errors of fact) that no serious scholar could mistake them for non-fiction. Daniel and Esther are about courage in face of the end of the world, and at the beginning of the revolt against Antiochus Epiphanes, things looked grim enough. The books of Maccabees are written in hindsight, and are not so apocalyptic. They tell how in the beginning a local Jewish family became the rulers of the Land of Israel, independent of the Seleucids for a century or so. They quarreled among themselves. What matters is that in 67 BCE, they invited the Romans in, to help settle their disputes, but the Romans took over.

The Romans were not nice. Life under the Romans was not the time of peace and prosperity the Jewish leaders evidently expected when they invited the Romans to come in and keep the peace. Taxes were too high, but that was not the biggest problem. The Romans tended to mistreat people, and they copied from the Assyrians of centuries before a particularly cruel method of eliminating trouble-makers: crucifixion.

When the Second Temple was built, and the idolatries of the Monarchy were eliminated, people expected a time of plenty and of freedom to worship their own peculiar God without interference from foreigners. It didn't work out that way. They were in the promised *land*, but they were not in the promised *time*. So the ingredients were there for a lot of discontent.

Being a people committed to living in history, they asked themselves what had gone wrong. There were many answers. If you would only keep the Law better, more faithfully, then God would throw the Romans out. (These were the Pharisees.) If you would do this, if you would do that. And so on. Maybe we should rise up and revolt, again; after all, the Maccabees succeeded, why can't we? God helped them, surely he will help us win against the Romans? (These were the Zealots.) Or we (we few, as it happened) should retire into the desert to pray, and let the world go to hell in a handbasket, as it seems determined to do. (The Essenes, who left us the Dead Sea Scrolls.) Or just be sensible and make the obvious compromises with the occupying power and get on with your life. (The Sadducees.) There were yet more varieties of Judaism in the Diaspora, the Jewish communities dispersed throughout the Roman Empire, particularly in Alexandria and Egypt, but also in Greece and in Mesopotamia, the last beyond the reach of the Romans.

4.6 The Disasters of the First Century

The idea of the Exodus as it grew when the first Temple was destroyed was a learning experience. Human life in history is to be affirmed, but to do that, two things are required. (These two of the seven lessons are the most important.) First, there has to be some kind of transcendence, because the pains of life hurt too much to affirm life in spite of them in the way you would brush off a bruised knee. The name for that transcendence is 'God.' The idea of God was not a problem for them as it has become one for us.

The second requirement was some way to live this commitment. World-affirming historical religion needs to be concrete, it needs to have a way to decide how to live according to a covenant in history. It doesn't happen in some abstract place. It takes more than just a few words about affirming life in history. It takes culture.

So how do you do it? And why isn't it working? People asked how to continue the Exodus covenant, in this the time of Julius Caesar, Caesar Augustus (and more provincially), King Herod and Quirinius, governor of Syria. They thought they knew what to do (keep the Law), and thought they just weren't doing a very good job of it. Psalm 119, the great acrostic poem about the Law, celebrates the divine commands from an earlier and happier age. Psalm 143 touches the nerve of the distress of Judaism in the First Century: "show me the road that I must walk, for I lift up my soul to you." What are we supposed to do? In hindsight, Psalm 119 seems to speak only for the Synagogue, for out of its questions, taken at face value, grows the Talmud. But it speaks for the predicament of the Church just as much, if less obviously, and not so literally.

More changes than meet the eye were happening in the first century of what later became known as "Anno Domini," under Christian influence. Today it is just the "Common Era," a calendar that cannot practically be changed but which needs a name that is not dismissive of rabbinic Judaism or other religions. In the time of the first Caesars, the transition from Roman Republic to the Empire, life and culture were problematic in the east end of the Mediterranean, the Land of Israel. It was not just the troubles with Rome, though they get most of the space in history books. Israelite religion had come a long way, and it really was not obvious how to continue. Whether to continue was never in doubt—but how? In the question whose answer the psalm presupposes, what are we supposed to do? What are we doing? What does it mean to live this way? These are not the words they used. Such questions are contemporary questions, questions that *we* ask, for in our own time we, too, are in doubt about our religion, how to understand it, and what this kind of religion really means.

We don't know with much confidence what happened at the Exodus, but it seems safe that the Jewish writers after the Exile *thought* they knew what happened in the Exodus, for they tell us, in texts that we have. Today, it seems likely enough that the time of the Exodus saw a move, subtle enough at first, from a religion of nature to a religion of history. During the time of the monarchy, it was mixed intimately with the surrounding nature religions, and indeed, seemed one of them—at first. Then after the disasters of the Exile, Israelite religion became the first real Judaism, the Judaism of the Second Temple. It succeeded in purging itself of at least the most visible signs of naturalistic religion, the idols and the names of the gods and goddesses that the idols represented.

A philosopher today would say that that merely poses the problem, without solving it: How is a historical religion supposed to work?

They tell us God *spoke* to them, laid down laws, and so on. Those texts may have been spoken and then written in a figurative sense, in the analogies we use casually when we know that figurative language in face-to-face conversation will not be misinterpreted. Later on, when only texts survived, and it was a question of God speaking to someone *else*, it was hard not to take the texts literally. And behind it all stands the notion of "God," unexamined. We shall come to that problem only after a good deal more history; it was not a question ripe for asking in the first century. What we can say today (section 8.4) does not really satisfy our craving for answers.

As the texts have it, God promised that if they kept the laws, things would go well for them, and if they didn't, things would go badly. (Deuteronomy is full of such promises.) But they were trying their best to keep the laws, and things still went badly. It was not working. There are two ways to respond: try harder, or ask what they were really supposed to be doing. People tried harder. And they did ask. In answer, there were many varieties of Judaism with various interpretations of what they were supposed to do.

The political disasters are simple enough to recount: the oppression by the Romans, culminating in the destruction of the Temple in 70 CE. And if there was any doubt, it was obliterated in the last of the disasters (a little into the second century, the end of the long tale of woe): In the year 132, the Jews revolted again, led by Simon Bar Kochba. In that revolt a great teacher and theologian died, rabbi Akiba. From the death of Jesus to the death of rabbi Akiba is about a century, and it was a time of one disaster after another. It's easy enough to call that time the Disasters of the First Century, even though the numbers are off by thirty years or so.

The Romans not only suppressed the rebellion in 135, they expelled the Jews from Jerusalem and erected a new temple where the old one had stood, this one to Jupiter, a Roman god—and an abomination from the point of view of the Jews. It was like not just burning down your house, but turning your lot into a public open-pit latrine afterward. After 135, it was completely clear that there was no going back to the Temple and its sacrifice.

If it were not for the disasters, Jewish religion would doubtless have continued pretty much as before. As it was, people had to stop and think, and they had to improvise in the aftermath. They couldn't make the Temple and its sacrifice central to their religion, because the Temple was gone. And Jews everywhere made the Temple central, not just those in the Land of Israel. For a self-respecting Jew would hope to go on pilgrimage to worship in the Temple eventually, even if he lived across the sea or across the desert. Many did. Paul did, in Acts 21, and we may assume that other Christians did as well.

4.7 Exodus, Again

The followers of Jesus grew quickly in the years right after his death. Perhaps not a large number of people, but certainly the movement was widespread, with churches in many cities in the Empire. The letters of Paul tell us that much. Before the destruction of the Temple in the year 70, it was just another sectarian group within first-century Judaism, somewhat fractious and quarrelsome among other groups. Not particularly out of the ordinary: Jews have always disagreed about how to be Jewish (as have Christians, about how to be Christian, right from the beginning).

The destruction of the Temple in 70 CE put them all to the question: how do you want to continue, without the Temple? The Jesus movement answered that in its own way. We are so used to the story in the Gospels that we take it as first, before the letters of Paul, and read Paul in the light of the Gospels. It was not that way at the time. The Church had to answer the question, how do you want to remember Jesus? What was he, for you? It had to answer his question, "Whom do you say that I am?" The answer is not as obvious as it seems. The Church wrote the Gospels in reply to this challenge. The creativity of the Gospel writers takes a little explaining, and scholars did not really appreciate it until recently.

People noticed already in the nineteenth century that the New Testament relies heavily on the Old, though this was not always seen positively. The twentieth century broadened its appreciation of how much the New builds on the Old. The New Testament alludes to the Old frequently. Some allusions are labeled. There are many quotations. And sometimes the Gospels trust readers to know and recognize the inherited Scripture in the very structure of the new story.

Consider: Both Jesus and the original Israelites, the family of Jacob, go down into Egypt. (Jesus was an infant, carried by his parents fleeing Herod's murderous wrath, and Jacob and family followed his son Joseph, who had been sold into Egypt by his brothers.) There is a slaughter of innocents in both stories (Herod's slaughter of the infants in Bethlehem, and Pharaoh's slaughter of the Hebrew male-children.) Both are tested and fed in the desert, one for forty days, the other for forty years. Both cross the Jordan river at Jericho. And both spend some time in the land and then go up to Jerusalem, David to conquer it, and Jesus, in an ironic sense, also to "conquer."

English departments usually are better at noticing such things, and they think it important when they do. It is like Monty Python's *Life of Brian*, fairly funny even for those who don't know the Gospels, but riotous for those who do. This parallel is not an accident. The idea is that Jesus is the new Israel, sometimes an individual, sometimes a whole people, just like the Servant Songs in Isaiah. We saw the four Servant Songs in Isaiah, and sometimes they are about an individual, sometimes the Servant of the Lord is the whole people. But the big story is not in Isaiah, though the Gospel writers occasionally borrow from Isaiah to interpret Jesus' death. The big story is in the Exodus: It was in the Exodus that Israel became a people, that the promises to the Patriarchs were fulfilled: land to live in, lots of children, and freedom to worship without interference from the Pharaohs of the world. That is merely to retell the story as it appears in the texts. There is more, as we shall see, for from the point of view of history of religions scholarship, the Exodus was a great watershed, even if one not noticeable as spectacular. For in the Exodus a people left nature religions and moved into history. This we have seen already. It is enough for now that the Judaisms of the first century, the Judaisms at the end of the Second Temple period, knew their own roots in the Exodus. At the Exodus, we became a real people, at the Exodus, we were given the Promised Land, and for the Exodus we are supposed to be grateful. When our neighbors thank the gods of nature for the harvest, we thank the Lord of History for the land in which we enjoy the harvest.

Our neighbors try to fit into *nature* naturally, but we want to be in a relationship with a great Mystery that lives behind the events of *history*.

In a relationship, two people or two parties make a commitment to each other. They called this relationship a *Covenant*, as we saw in chapter 3. They had models, in the diplomatic treaties of an earlier age, wherein a Hittite overlord promised to protect and defend a vassal city in return for the vassal's obedience and loyalty. The upshot of a covenant is that the two parties travel through history together, and the Lord of History will take care of the human partners in the covenant. The focus of the covenant had always been the sacrifices in the Temple. That's what made it concrete, that's what made it real.

Now look at the situation of the first "Christians"—still Jews, really, part of the wider confusion among the Judaisms of the first century. This was *before* the revolt of 67-73 CE and the destruction of the Temple in 70 CE. This is the "Christianity" of Paul, quarrelsome among the Jews, but one of them still. In the hindsight of later events, these quarrels will be transformed into the beginning of another religion, but that hasn't happened yet. Remember, Paul went to great trouble to carry money, alms and gifts, to the people in the Land of Israel, and when he got there, he went to the Temple. That's how he got into the trouble that sent him to Rome in chains, where according to legend, he was martyred. So the Temple was still the center of the Jewish world, even for the first Christians.

What do you do when the Temple is gone, really gone? When the Temple no longer can be the center of your religion? You have to reinvent it, and you have to retell the story to do that. That's how the Gospels came to be written, and that's why the Gospels are a parody of the Exodus. It's a way to tell the reader that what happened at the Exodus has happened again, in our time, and for us.

The word *parody* is not exactly right, but it is the word we know. Usually in a parody, the older text is being ridiculed; here it is revered. The proper technical term for the biblical relation of the later to the earlier is *typology*: the earlier is a type of the later. But that terminology is so unfamiliar that we shall often speak of parody instead, remembering that this is parody with reverence, not parody with derision. The language of typology was familiar for many centuries.

Before, when there was a Temple, there were sacrifices in the Temple, and those sacrifices were *the* central religious observance. At Passover, the lambs in Jerusalem were sacrificed by priests, in the Temple. Now what do you do? In a re-invention of the Temple, Jesus' death became for these people the Passover sacrifice, and its re-enactment in the common meal made that sacrifice present to people in the here and now. "Christ our Passover is sacrificed for us: Therefore let us keep the feast." The text (1 Cor 5.7) is Pauline, well before the destruction of the Temple, so the idea was not new in the aftermath of disaster. But it was built up into something new, and something much bigger, after the disaster. Paul's short phrase became the passion stories in the Gospels, and the passion stories grew into a retelling of the Exodus.

4.8 Jesus

The idea of a new Exodus was itself not new: deutero-Isaiah used it long before to explain the return from bondage in the Exile in Babylon. The Gospel writers used it again. If Jesus is the new Joshua, leading the people of a new Exodus into a new covenant, what, exactly, is this new covenant? That question has many answers, and I would like to select only a few of them, without any claim of generality or comprehensiveness. The features we need in order to make sense of our predicament in Christianity today are fairly simple. They are also less surprising than is Exodus typology. The organization follows the work of Edward Hobbs. What Jesus offers is in the teaching, the miracles, and the Passion. That much is not new.

Here are some of the themes of the teaching of Jesus: (1) Repent! The jig is up, it's time to change your ways, you're about to be caught red-handed! (2) Quit complaining, stop making invidious comparisons with your neighbor, and accept life in gratitude and joy. And lastly, (3), love (which is to say, help) your neighbor in need. If you do these things, you will enter into the life promised in the Exodus covenant, as it continues after the first century, without the Land and the Temple. This much is from Hobbs's teaching materials, unpublished though they be.

A few examples will suffice. Repentance is announced at the beginning of the first Gospel: "... The kingdom of God is close at hand. Repent, ..." (Mark 1:15, paralleled in Matthew 3:2). Repentance (unnamed) is the prerequisite for the wedding feast in Matthew 22. Luke is full of examples of those who do repent—and those who don't.

The call to repentance is echoed many times, not least in the healings, as we shall see. It was a theme in the air everywhere in first-century Palestinian Judaism: if we repent, perhaps God will restore us to independence and freedom (cf. p. 68, about Psalm 119). It is no surprise that Jesus breathed that air. The Gospel writers took the theme and made something more of it. It continues, by the way, as an enduring theme in rabbinic Judaism: *shuv*, repentance.

The most famous polemic against envy and ingratitude is in Matthew 20, the laborers in the vineyard. They are all paid the same wages, even though some worked the whole day, and others only an hour at the end. Jesus tells them to quit complaining.

Injunctions to help one's neighbor abound. The good Samaritan (Luke 10) is only the best known; Zacchaeus' alms for the poor (Luke 19) is another. Luke is especially sensitive for the poor.

There is more, certainly, than this—the parable of the sower is about change of life, repentance, but it is also about the difficulty and subtlety and slowness of that change. The parables challenge at many levels: at the start, they want repentance, gratitude, and love. Beyond that, they want a transformation of life that can be quite hard to get control of. John is structured differently, and is focused more on the role of Jesus than on his teaching or miracles, but some of the same themes appear. The story of the man born blind (chapter 9) is about gratitude and ingratitude, and about recognizing the providence of God or missing it.

The themes of the teaching are repeated in the miracles, though it may take a little work to recognize them. As Edward Hobbs observed, Jesus cleanses, raises, and feeds Israel. Some healings are cleansings, some healings are raisings. The cleansings are implicit in the maladies healed: uncleanness of some kind (usually demon-possession or leprosy). The raisings are often labeled with the verb for raising, *egeiro*. Impurity (and disability more generally) were taken as a symptom of sin (John 9:2, the man born blind), even though Jesus doesn't always interpret it that way. The cleansings are the counterpart of the call to repentance, the healing of sin (i. e., forgiveness). Indeed, in our haste to get to the cure, we don't notice the times when, as prolog to the healing, the patient repents, or has his or her sins forgiven. The paralytic's sins are forgiven (Mark 2:5) before he is raised. It is not an invariable part of the stories, but it occurs often enough so that, once spotted, it stands out. For us, it is odd: we don't keep a priest in a confessional booth at the door of the hospital emergency room.

We find the miracle texts very disturbing, because we tend to see the special effects and think we have to believe them literally or not at all. We know how to *read* the miracle texts "literally," whether we *believe* them literally or not. Indeed, when Peter Jackson turned the *Lord of the Rings* books into action movies, he assumed his audience would recognize the New Testament miracle genre when Gandalf expels the influence of the wizard Saruman from Théoden king of Rohan. Gandalf flexes his staff and speaks harshly, Théoden is convulsed (cf. Mark 1:26), and the figure of Saruman is cast out—passively, on Théoden's part. (*Two Towers*, CD number 1, at 1h 19m – 1h 21m)

In the book, things are more mundane. There are few special effects—a little sound and light, but no convulsions or visible demons expelled. Gandalf merely persuades, and Théoden finds his courage and his better judgement, and so changes his ways (p. 119). In the book, we have the repentance, and in the movie, the grander special effects—without the repentance nobody understands anyway. Peter Jackson counts on his viewers knowing how healing miracles go—with special effects, literally—and without the messiness of repentance. We are willing to suspend normal criteria of what can happen and what cannot when watching *The Lord of the Rings*, but we are unwilling, or don't know what to do, when reading the Gospel miracle stories.

The literal interpretation of the miracle stories is inconsistent with the teaching of Jesus, which advocates change of life in at least three ways, but does not offer magical changes to passive believers. Perhaps Romans 8:28, an earlier text, can help us here: St. Paul says, "by turning everything to their good God co-operates with all those who love him," as it is in the Jerusalem Bible. The King James has "all things work together for good to them that love God." The Jerusalem Bible makes both God and the faithful more active in the events. (And if it is passive gratuitous healing, why heal some and not others, or why not just heal everybody, wholesale? The problems of a literal reading are insurmountable.)

If we have trouble suspending disbelief in the miracle texts, we have no trouble at all in another kind of modern miracle story, television advertisements. (Edward Hobbs saw that, cf. p. 158 below.) The preposterous regularly happens, even the unphysical, and we know it is all in the service of selling a product. So what product are the Gospel miracle texts selling? That would be in the teaching—an invitation to embrace exposure, limitation, and need as they meet you in life. Exposure is embraced (or preemptively avoided) in repentance. Limitation is embraced in giving up envy and working with what you have. Need is embraced in love of neighbor. We saw them first on p. 6, but there without their roots in the Gospels. If they really do bring good, then by turning everything to their good God really does co-operate with all those who love him. We began with these three pains of life, and with the blessings they bear. They are the key to many puzzles. They hold the story together.

Chapter 5

Biblical Religion in Late Antiquity

5.1 The Survivors

There were a number of responses to the disasters of the first century. One was retreat from the world, confident that the world was coming to an end soon anyway, and that it would be replaced by a Messiah sent to set things right. That was the way of Qumran, the monastery in the salt desert by the Dead Sea. The world didn't come to an end, they did. Someone (the Romans, who else?) suppressed the community, destroyed their buildings, and doubtless killed them. What did they do to annoy? It can't have been hard.

The way of escape from the world always appeals. Some seek escape with imprecations directed at the world they have left behind, like the people at Qumran. They went away mad, full of vituperation and curses. This we know because shortly before the Romans destroyed them, they left a cache of scrolls hidden in pottery jars in the caves high up on the cliffs above their community. Those scrolls are known as "The Dead Sea Scrolls," a priceless literary treasure offering a window into an obscure side of first century Judaism. If the disciples of Qumran retreated into anger, others took an easier route, less confrontational. They were known as Gnostics, and I come to them in a moment.

The Sadducees were the ruling establishment in Palestinian Judaism, and they were noted for not believing in the resurrection, and perhaps for not being as observant as (say) the Pharisees. The Sadducees' version of the story of the Maccabees, which we have noticed already, doesn't mention God even once. It is hard to see how you could make a religion out of such a way of life—certainly not a religion that would offer much help or comfort to people other than the rich. This, too, is a lifestyle that has parallels enough today.

Another legacy of the Second Temple period was the Jewish community descended from the Babylonian captivity, flourishing in Persia. Lost to the Mediterranean world, it rejoins our story later, in the Talmuds.

At some distance, well beyond the land of Israel but in a large Jewish community, was Philo, a philosopher and biblical scholar in Alexandria. He probably didn't read Hebrew very well, but he was well read in Greek. Plato was the dominant philosopher of the culture. To be serious about philosophy or religion in Alexandria meant engaging Plato. The writings of Philo that we have portray the Bible as Plato's source, which makes the Bible better than Plato. Philo corrects Plato where he must, assimilates him where he can. In the end, the writings of Philo were preserved by the Church and not the Synagogue. Christian theologians liked Plato a lot better than the rabbis did. The Church fathers may have thought Philo a Christian; his work was certainly congenial to Christian theology. Philo can stand as one example of how "far out" Judaism could be in the first century.

The Zealots were the ones who thought they could bring in the Messianic time by their own efforts. They, too, are typical of a perennial view, the temptation to think a perfect world can be made in the here and now. Parallels in the modern world abound. But the Zealots were the rebels in 67–73 and 132–135 CE, and they were obliterated by the Romans.

Let me come to Gnostic groups last, and deal next with the Pharisees. Both Jesus and the rabbis were of this party. The writers put harsh words on Jesus's lips toward the Pharisees in the Gospels, but he was one of them. People spend most of their energy disagreeing with their closest neighbors; those obviously wrong can be ignored or dismissed.

The story branches shortly, for only the Pharisees (the Jesus movement and the rabbis) survived in the long run. The Zealots and Essenes were destroyed violently. And the Sadducees? Who would sympathize with the established leadership of a subject people crushed in a rebellion? They were eliminated in any case. Philo and people like him were not so far as I know ever really a movement organized for worship, and so not a movement that could attract large numbers of people other than philosophers. (And how many philosophers were there? Probably not many.) The Jesus movement and the rabbis soon went in different directions, but they (or their heirs) had significant features in common, features worth noting in advance.

They both continued the Exodus tradition in a recognizable but changed form. They both affirmed life in this world in varying degrees. It may not seem that way, for the earliest Christians thought the world would end soon; they were heirs of apocalyptic movements in Judaism. Nevertheless, the Christians in the end affirmed human life in this world, as we shall see when we come to Augustine. The Church and the Synagogue are both examples of a world-affirming historical religion, however much they may from time to time have made compromises with world-denying ideas. They both found ways of holding people responsible. That is necessary for the social and spiritual welfare of the community and for the integrity of the concepts that keep it together. They both maintained a focus of identity in the absence of the Temple: Christ for one group, and the Law (most obviously kashrut, the kosher food laws), for the other group. They both maintained a vigorous life of prayer and with it a viable worship in place of the lost worship in the Temple. In both cases, worship became congregational, that is, an activity of people meeting together in large groups to sing, read, and pray. This was a new model for worship: the older model was one in which a few at a time would come as clients to the priests in the Temple to sacrifice animals for their own personal needs.

In another big change, at about this time in the history of the eastern Mediterranean, there began to appear groups who later were called "Gnostics." They believed that this material world, and especially the human body in it, are defective, a kind of prison. You are really supposed to be just a spirit, and you want to escape from the body as fast as you can, and get back to being just a spirit. That, however, requires knowledge, for if you don't know how to do it, you can't succeed. *Gnosis* means knowledge, and Gnostics believed in salvation by knowledge.

There were many Gnostic groups, and some of the Gnostic ideas are older than Plato. Indeed, Plato in the West is the most visible spokesman for the idea that human beings are composed of a body and a soul and that the soul is detachable from the body. In Israelite religion (and in Homeric religion as well), a human being is an integral unity, and the idea of separation of soul from body is never contemplated in quite the way that Platonists developed it later. Clearly, Gnosticism requires something like this if it plans to escape from the body and the physical world.

What it also needed was a source of knowledge, and that source was supposed to be a person, a Gnostic redeemer sent from higher realms to impart the necessary knowledge to those who were smart enough to understand. The masses, people of low culture, aren't smart enough. If you can follow the directions, you can get your soul out of the body when you die, and return to those higher realms, mingle with the spirit-lords there, and eventually return to be one with the deity. (If you fail, you will be reincarnated and imprisoned in a new body all over again.) What Gnostics were *not* interested in was repentance, for they did not take the biblical notion of sin seriously. And they were not interested in history, because history is part of this world, and this world is a total loss.

How were Gnostics supposed to make sense of the creation stories in the Bible, in Genesis? This world was created by an incompetent and malicious being, one less than the full divinity. Thus was the God of Genesis and the Jewish scriptures dismissed. For Genesis 1 had seven times declared this world to be good, even very good; not at all the way Gnostics saw things.

There were many Gnostic groups, and sometimes it is hard to tell whether they were "Jewish" or "Christian" or just Gnostic without biblical overtones. In later centuries, some of the Gnostic ideas stayed with the Church, clearly, and even with the Synagogue, if less clearly. Platonism was adopted by both the Church and the Synagogue in varying degrees, and Platonism provides the raw ingredients out of which you can "roll your own" Gnosticism. That part of the story will not be very surprising.

What is surprising is how the first Christian writers after Paul saw their movement.

5.2 A Parting of the Ways

The idea that the Gospels are a parody of the Exodus is not intuitively obvious today, no matter how strong the parallels in the two narratives are. More likely people focus on the split between Christianity and Judaism in the first century, which is well known. (Actually, it took longer than that. The separation was not final until the fourth century.) How it happened is not nearly as obvious as it once was.

The two usual versions of the story are not entirely satisfying. According to a common Christian account, the Jews rejected Jesus, and so God disinherited them. This unsavory perspective was nearly universal until recently. According to a reciprocal Jewish account, Christianity arose as an entirely new religion, and the fact that its first members were Jews should not obscure the reality that it has very little to do with Judaism. And so each religion had its own rhetoric for disinheriting the other from whatever legitimacy could be scraped together out of the ashes of the Second Temple. Things deteriorated as the centuries passed. The antipathy of later centuries is read back into the New Testament documents in support of both of these stories.

There has been a lot of writing (and soul-searching) among scholars recently about the parting of the ways between Christianity and rabbinic Judaism, and it will doubtless go on for some time yet. I would like to focus on retelling the story of the career of world-affirming historical religion, and how it survives intact and whole in *both* daughter religions.

The outcome of the fighting between proto-Christians and proto-rabbis and their respective congregations was not entirely pretty. What they *said* to each other, in effect, was something like this:

"You rejected The Law (God's Law!)."

"You rejected The Messiah (God's Messiah!)."

But in reality, what each *felt* toward the other was more like, "you rejected *our* way of continuing the covenant." Our messiah; our law. Oh, how it hurts when we try to help God, and we are rejected! It was our gift to God, but in our hurt and anger, it is easy to think it is God's gift to us that those evil other people have rejected. And then, of course, we would have to face our own responsibility and creativity in our own religious choices, and that would cost us some anxiety. A *lot* of anxiety.

Some errors can be ruled out at the start. Jesus was *not* rejected by his people; they opened their hearts and their homes to him. And the pharisees were not doing a theology of "works righteousness." Though we can't go into details here, it is clear enough to scholars that the pharisees were just as interested in repentance and forgiveness as Jesus was. A later rabbinic text has it that repentance was among the six things created before the creation of the world. The idea that pharisaic Judaism was a religion of works-righteousness got about when the Reformers read Paul. Their real target was abuses in the

Catholic Church of the fifteenth and sixteenth centuries, and Judaism got tarred with Paul's brush along the way. But the Judaism of the Talmuds was so open to grace offered for repentance that a man was saved after his *son* repented on his behalf by saying the Mourner's Kaddish after he died (Hertz, p. 271). Talk about sinners getting into heaven free!

And the Gospel of John notwithstanding, there were voices on behalf of caution and forbearance in both proto-Christianity and among the pharisees. The quotation of rabbi Gamaliel in Acts 5.34 ff. is well known. He said that the Jesus movement might be a work of God, and opposition to it should not assume to know exhaustively what God has planned. Less obvious are chapters 9-11 in Romans. Paul is by no means sweet on the Synagogues of his time (as Gamaliel in turn was not sweet on the first followers of Jesus). But Paul is also quite clear to his readers that Israel (the people that would later be rabbinic Judaism) was not rejected. Romans 11.1 is clear and explicit and I don't see how you can weasel out of it. "Let me put a further question then: is it possible that God has rejected his people? Of course not."

Later in the chapter, he says, "The Jews are enemies . . . only with regard to the Good News, and enemies only for your own sake." At the three dots in this quotation, some modern translations have inserted "of God," making the Jews enemies *of God*, a translation that is completely unjustified (see Norman Beck). (Almost all older translations got it right, even Luther, who didn't much like Jews.) The extra words are just not in the Greek text, and to put them there is anti-Jewish theology. If the sentence is read as it really is, what it means, from a later perspective, is that the Church needs the Synagogue to be strong, healthy, and different, because the Synagogue keeps us honest. Rabbinic Judaism of course has bigger and better reasons for existing than just to keep the Church honest. Paul's message here is one good reason for the Church to honor the Synagogue rather than to reject it or claim to have superseded it.

Nevertheless, the split happened. What was going on? In our

terms, I would say they disagreed about what counts as a world-affirming historical religion. What makes your basic life orientation both world-affirming and historical? In their terms, the question was different. What counts as continuing the Exodus covenant as it was inherited from Second Temple Judaism? What do we have to do to continue (Second Temple) Judaism without the Temple? Their view of the issues has been preserved in language that comes down to us almost intact even into the twentieth century.

They asked about faithfulness to the unity of God, the identity of the covenant people, the scriptures, and the place of the Temple and its sacrifice. A very concrete way to ask about how to continue a covenant. There was little theory and less philosophy.

Clearly, there were frictions between Jesus and others in the pharisaic movement in Palestinian Judaism. Two things more or less insured that Jesus was not adopted by the leadership as messiah after he died. He was not part of the leadership before he died, nor was he really serving the leadership. That sort of outsider rarely becomes a hero. And Jesus came to a bad end. He lost. It is not surprising that the leadership was not impressed, and in fairness, you could hardly blame them.

In any case, through perceived and sometimes real differences about what it means to respect the oneness of God, the identity of the covenant people, the role of the Torah and the best course after the loss of the Temple, the Jesus movement and the pharisaic remnant, the rabbis, gradually parted company. They were not separated at the time of the first Jewish revolt, in 67–73 CE. There was considerable confusion and there were groups in between them until after 70 CE. By the teens of the second century, outsiders recognized Christians as a distinct group. (Pliny, for one; Justin Martyr, for another.) By 132–135, the split has appeared to later readers as more or less complete and probably irreparable. But recent work indicates that it was not final until the fourth century (Boyarin, 2004). This history is being revised at present; the shape of it is not entirely clear.

Return to the fifth of the lessons of the Exodus. I claimed that for covenantal religion, the God comes into the world to be with us in a world that is good, if painful, rather than to help us escape from an evil world. The goodness of the world is what the idea of creation is all about. This was only beginning to be an issue in a self-conscious or *theoretical* way when the Common Documents were put together, even though the goodness of the created world runs unlabeled through all the texts. There are only hints in Deuteronomy (30.11) and maybe a few other places. In the first century, the issues had changed. In the time of the Exodus itself, conjecturally, and the monarchy, more clearly, affirming this world was taken for granted, both in the nature religions and in the nascent historical religion. The issue in dispute was about history, the choice whether to live in a way that focuses on history, though of course, they rarely put it that way. The words the prophets put on the lips of God were, "I'm the one who brought you out of Egypt, but you forgot!" This is history without the name.

In the Hellenistic world, the world of multi-national empires ending in Roman domination and extreme cultural pluralism, there was a lot of doubt about how much to affirm life in this world as good. It is not at all obvious whether God comes into the world so we can get out of pain and history, out of the inherited mess and leave it behind, or whether God comes into history so we can continue an inherited covenant in a good world. The first, the world-rejecting interpretation, has all too often been the modern Christian view of God coming into the world in Jesus.

The second possibility, that God comes into the world to be with us in a good world, was much more central than one might think in the theology of both the Jesus movement and the first rabbis. But to do a world-affirming historical religion in real life requires some concrete and tangible focus. For one group, it was Christ, a historical person; for the other, it was kashrut, kosher food practices in the home. And in that choice, clear enough already in Paul's letters, the two groups split. Let me deal with them in turn in the next few sections. How things worked out in practice was much more complicated than this simple difference might suggest.

5.3 The First Christians

When Merold Westphal came to describe world-affirming historical religion (he called it "historical-covenantal religion") in *God, Guilt, and Death*, he covered the Common Documents and the New Testament. We will briefly note the Talmuds also. If you read between the lines, he was embarrassed when he came to the New Testament. For he had already laid out the story of Israelite religion as a pilgrimage through history in the company of the God, in a relationship of trust. The God comes into history to be with the covenant people in a good world. In the New Testament, all this is at risk, in doubt, for one can read the New Testament quite differently. Misread, it tells a story of the God coming into history to get us out of a bad world. Here, the body is evil and the spirit good, the church is the elite and the world is lost. One can read heaven as good in contrast to the earth as bad. This is so natural a reading, so common a reading in the last three or four hundred years, that to question it comes as a surprise.

Closer examination of the texts, in Westphal's tour of them, shows that vice lodges in the soul and spirit as much as in the flesh, and virtue can be found in both as well. Paul says the body is to be a temple of the Lord—hardly a rejection of the body. Heaven is to be a consummated earth, a rebuilt and perfected earth, not an escape from earth. And the church is to save the world, just as Abraham was to be a blessing to all peoples. But even if the New Testament is not really peddling a quasi-gnostic rejection of the body and the world, those ideas are widespread and attractive now. As it happens, they were widespread and attractive then, too.

These ideas we have seen in regard to Gnosticism, p. 81 above. In the Gnosticism of late antiquity, this world is evil, and the body is especially evil. It is all a prison for the soul. Gnosticism typically features a gnostic redeemer, a being sent from the higher realms to give the Gnostic elite the knowledge needed to get a soul out of all bodies and back to being a part of the godhead. Jesus was ready-to-hand and available for the job. The redemption from sin in the New Testament could be pushed in the direction of an escape from an evil world. That temptation has traveled with Christianity almost from the beginning.

Where did these ideas come from, in the Greco-Roman world? That is a good question, one without entirely obvious answers. Parts may have come from Persia, the religion of Zoroaster. Parts can be found in Plato. Parts could easily have come from India, but the evidence, though there is some, is thin. Zoroastrian religion sees a world radically divided between good and evil, with evil in danger of winning. Plato gives us a radical split between body and soul, and the soul is detachable from the body. In principle, the soul could live quite happily without a body, it doesn't really need a body at all. Plato's predecessors, the Orphics, Pythagoras and his students, had already conjured up the idea of reincarnation. They thought it was a perpetual re-imprisonment in an infinite series of bodies, each one as sick and hurting as the last. The Indian versions of all this are much more elaborate, and popular in America today.

It is easy to see how the New Testament could be read as a Gnostic collection. If one is not aware of the background in Jewish scriptures, the redeemer seems Gnostic enough: he came from somewhere else, and he promises help in the present pains. That must be help to get *out* of the pains of this world, right?

There's the rub: the Gospels were written as a reverent parody of the Exodus, but what about readers who don't know the story of the Exodus? (What do viewers who don't know the Gospels do with Monty Python's *Life of Brian*? I don't know.) You can tell newcomers, "We're the Jesus movement, and here's our story. And by the way, here's our *older* story, and you have to start with the older story. You need the older story to understand what happened recently." But the newcomers already had plenty of stories from the Hellenistic world.

They didn't need the Exodus story to make sense of Jesus. They could take Jesus as just another Hellenistic redeemer figure, come to save us from our pains, not from our sins. All too often unheard is the Gospel message that Jesus came to save us not *from* our pains but *in and by* our pains (and his).

The Hellenistic world was a riot of religious options: demons, magic, street philosophy, serious philosophy, astrology, the mystery religions, and various Gnostic groups. Stoics thought the world was a place of pain, but you could be brave and rise above it. Epicureans thought you might as well enjoy the world, and there was enough to enjoy. The mystery religions usually had a feminine savior (Mithraism was an exception), and by initiation into mystical knowledge, you could find your way through this life and eventually into another. Sounds like a stepping-stone to Gnosticism? It was. And there were remnants of the older religion of the great Greek gods, but reduced to a few observances at passages in life—very much like lapsed Catholics today who go to church only at Christmas and Easter and weddings, baptisms, and funerals. This is the counterpart of contemporary secular society, with echoes of piety but without much sustained effort or serious commitment. The parallels between Western culture today and the Hellenistic world run deep. In a society where religious options abound and all are plausible, none can enjoy self-evident truth. Smorgasbord religion becomes the theme of the culture.

For the most part, the concepts and idioms of the Hellenistic world were shared by all, Jews and Christians and everybody else alike. The heirs of the Bible dispute the culture in a few places, but they didn't dispute it everywhere. How could they? Biblical religion, moving out into the Hellenistic world, took over its ideas and idioms and spoke to it in its own terms. Remember the central idea in Deuteronomy 30.11, the idea that grows to animate all of world-affirming historical religion, that the God comes into the world to bless it, not to get us out of it. A good definition of incarnation says that, in incarnation, the God comes to you in the terms of your own time. That carries some hazards. From the point of view of history of religions, when a new religion moves into an older culture, it makes compromises with the older culture. Mongolian Buddhists eat meat, though the original Indian Buddhists did not. Chinese Buddhism took on much that is native to China, and left some things from its origins in India.

Compromise can be embarrassing for the theologian. It should not be. Compromise is not necessarily an unworthy sellout to the culture. To speak to your own culture, you have to speak its language at least some of the time, or else it will not hear. And the idea that the God blesses *this* world means that he blesses this culture. That's hard. Because it means he blesses sinners and sinful institutions and all their ideas with them. Not to say they are right in their sins, not to say their sins are excused. But the repentance, the conversion of life, will take a long time. Centuries. Maybe millennia.

One indication that the Christians in the second and third centuries were not just another Hellenistic mystery religion is that they were not seen that way. They were seen as freaks, sociopaths who wouldn't cooperate with the general attitude of mutual toleration between different religions in the Roman Empire. Like the Jews, they refused to reciprocate respect for other religions' rituals. They refused the right sort of reverence for the Emperor. And so they were persecuted. Speak the language of the culture though they did, they still challenged the culture. They were understood as a challenge, clearly. One too disturbing to allow.

5.4 Thomas and Marcion

The nineteenth-century historians discovered to their surprise that "heresy is older than orthodoxy" in the history of earliest Christianity. People saw many different things in Jesus; that much is clear even in Acts. Some of them ended up in the Church, some did not. There were many versions of Christianity at the beginning, and a semblance of order came only belatedly. That order came because people wanted it, I suppose; at least some did. The others went their own way. They left texts enough, a small crowd of other gospels, epistles, apocalypses, and so on, both like and unlike the documents we have in the standard New Testament.

The most famous and most widely read today is the Gospel of Thomas. It was cited often enough in ancient literature, but no text was available until recently. The Nag Hammadi library, discovered in the late 1940s, has a complete text. The Gospel of Thomas gets attention because it reads easily, and scholars think there may be some genuine sayings of Jesus in it. It has no narrative, no Passion, no healings; only teaching. The flavor is noticeably different from the teaching in the canonical Gospels, and you might have a hard time putting your finger on just why that is. It is more "laid back," less in-your-face. It is for those in the know. It puts a different spin on some of the same ideas, subtle and surreptitious at first, insidious as you read on, but quite different in the end. And it doesn't have the radical edge of the canonical Gospels: little repentance, no confronting the pains as part of a good life and world, and no helping others when it hurts. It has no apocalyptic message about the end of the world, either. Jesus is a teacher of wisdom, without the hard stuff. It's easy to like. After all, the message is that you're all right, you're really divine, you just don't know it yet.

Another movement in the second century profoundly changed the life of the church. It is closer to Thomas than to the fully developed Gnostic cosmological speculations. A second century priest named Marcion was the leader of the movement. Marcion was repudiated by the Church, but the Church adopted some of his program nonetheless.

Marcion grew up in Asia Minor, was excommunicated by his father, a bishop, for immorality, came to Rome in about 140 CE, and died about 160. He was excommunicated (apparently for the second time) in 144, when he had organized a movement of his own. The movement spread over most of the Roman Empire. The main idea was that the original gospel is only about love; there is nothing about law in it at all. This sounds very Pauline, and Marcion liked the epistles of Paul.

He is best known for what he did next. He got rid of the "Old Testament." After all, the God of the Old Testament is just a God of law, and so a God of wrath and punishment. There is no love or forgiveness there. Not at all the God whom Jesus came to reveal. (Occasionally someone will earnestly feed me this line today, unaware of where it came from.)

Marcion didn't much like Gnosticism, especially its complicated speculations about cosmic hierarchies of mystical beings. He gets classed with the Gnostics because he shared their dislike of law, and because he shared their dislike of the Common Documents. And he was anti-Jewish in a way that went far beyond what the orthodox Christian writers ever said.

Marcion liked Paul, at least the passages about gospel and law and liberation from the Law. Unlike many readers today, Marcion could recognize the heritage of the Common Documents in most of the Gospels. He kept only an edited version of Luke, trashing Matthew, Mark, and John entirely. (How he missed the Jewish side of Luke is a good question, when he saw it well enough in the other three. But I don't know what parts of Luke he kept.)

Marcion edited a *collection* of Christian documents, and that poses a challenge, raises the question for the rest of the Church: What collection do you (or anyone else) want to keep? What's in, what's out, what's orthodox, what's heretical, what's old and authoritative, what's nice but just derivative? Approximately the New Testament that we have came out of the Marcionite crisis. Hebrews and Revelation were added later. The result of the crisis was an agreed collection of central orthodox texts, a *standard* for judging other writing. The Greek word for standard is *canon*.

But the challenge was more than just about New Testament documents. For what do you do about the inherited scripture? What is its status? After Marcion?

What the Church did is not entirely pretty. In order to meet Marcion, it conceded too much to him. For it downgraded the Common Documents, and they became the "Old" Testament, as in Obsolete Testament. Not uncanonical, not out of the Bible, but superseded. Good for prophecies that get fulfilled in the New Testament, in contrast to the prototype of salvation that we have seen mirrored in the structure of the Gospels. It was no longer *the* story of the history of salvation. That begins with Jesus. Whenever people think that "in the beginning was Jesus," it is because of the Church's compromising response to Marcion that they can talk that way. To be fair, Christians continued to *read* the Common Documents until the modern world. When the monks and the clergy chant the Exodus story once every Friday and twice on Saturday in Psalms 78 and 105–106, it is hard to forget completely. (The Exodus runs through many other Psalms as well, but in these three, it is the theme.) Nevertheless, they didn't put much weight on the Common Documents theologically, and didn't much treasure the history in them. Only in the modern world has Marcionite theology returned overtly, and we shall come to that on p. 164. Christians often don't even read the Common Documents. The Vatican II lectionary sought to reverse that trend, mandating that a lesson from the Old Testament be read at every Mass.

The response to Marcion is one root of what has recently been called "supersessionism," the idea that the Church supersedes Judaism, which is disinherited from God's love and favor. There are roots enough of supersessionist theology among Christians earlier than Marcion, but this is where it all congeals into the ugly mess of anti-Jewish theology that we know today, and are only now beginning to dismantle.

Two sad things came out of the compromises with Marcion. The Church weakened its loyalty to the Common Documents, and ceased to put much theological weight on them beyond using prophecies as proof-texts to validate the New Testament. The second thing that happened was that the split between the Church and the Synagogue was radically deepened. It became a Great Exclusive Or: only one of us can be right, only one of us can legitimately inherit from Second Temple Judaism.

One very good thing came out of the Marcionite crisis: The Church did not concede all to Marcion, and in what she kept there was something very precious, beyond just the Common Documents themselves. The Greek and Latin Church kept a sense of indebtedness to the Jews, and so to a "foreign" culture. That sense of not being the center of the religious world grew by stages. In the Latin West, the Church also kept a sense of being indebted to the Greeks. That was more than just to the Greek Church; it was a debt also to the Greek philosophers. Roman culture had such a sense of indebtedness, and the Church preserved it. The Latin West could view none of her religious treasures as her own by birthright. In the words of Rémi Brague (2002), she preserved a sense of being eccentric, not at the center. That grew into an openness to other cultures more generally.

5.5 Constantine and the Talmuds

My limited observations of a kosher kitchen have been entirely positive. At night before going to bed, I generally go round the house and turn off lights, and found the oven on one Friday night, left on by one of my tenants. The second time it happened, I had the sense to leave it as I found it. It is kosher to warm food in an oven on the sabbath, but not kosher to turn the oven on.

What was happening was something beautiful and holy. I could interfere with it, perhaps, but not really participate, because I'm not Jewish. It is a way to sanctify life at one of its crossroads: eating, where life is sustained by food. There are other crossroads, and the Torah, as it comes to us interpreted in the Talmuds, sanctifies them all. Birth, death, sex, marriage, and food are the most visible. Other transactions are regulated, too, and because these are repeated places in life, they take on a special significance. Blessings are prescribed.

The *way* to do things is prescribed. The first tractate in the Talmud is about blessings for all the various occasions in life. In a word, it all works to make sure you remember that this is supposed to be a world-*affirming* religion.

How did it all get started? That's complicated, especially for Christian readers. Clearly, some of it dates from the Second Temple period, for it was an issue of controversy in the New Testament. But the texts are younger than that, coming from the second century of the common era and later.

Let me come to the history of the texts in a moment. For now, it is enough to know that the original rabbinic document is the Mishnah, 700–1000 pages in various translations, and it was edited by one rabbi Judah, apparently around the year 200 CE, though a few parts of it may be later than that. After the Mishnah comes a great deal of secondary literature, until there are two encyclopedia-sized commentaries on it, the two Talmuds. The Mishnah is a collection of legal rules, arranged into six Orders, dealing with six different areas of life.

We owe much of our English-language access to these texts to Jacob Neusner, an American scholar working in the second half of the twentieth century. He taught at Brown University and eventually moved to Florida, as people from New England sometimes do. He has almost single-handedly translated both Talmuds, the Mishnah and related rabbinic literature, as well as produced countless volumes of reflection on it all. He is not the only one who has seen the creativity of the first rabbis, but he is one of the more conspicuous voices: rabbinic Judaism can stand on its own documents as a religion of great beauty and faith. Not without the Torah, but not limited to the Torah and the Common Documents, either. Without the rabbinic literature, Judaism (and the world) would be much poorer. It is possible now, in English, to deal with texts that were obscure or unavailable until recently. It is possible for mere goyim illiterate in Hebrew to see the treasures of the Synagogue, and that largely through Jacob Neusner's work.

One of the six orders of the Mishnah is about cleanness and uncleanness, principally of food, what may be eaten and what may not, and how it may be prepared. Jacob Neusner wrote a long commentary called *A History of the Mishnaic Law of Purities* to try to reconstruct how it was put together. It is not unusual for a culture to define some foods as clean and others as unclean. In the ancient world most did, and some still do today. For only one example, though Americans usually won't eat dog or monkey meat, some other cultures do. When the leaders of the kingdom of Judah were deported to Babylon in 586 BCE, many stayed there, and there was a Jewish community in Mesopotamia from that time until quite recently. (Middle Eastern politics in the twentieth century has pretty much evacuated Arab countries of their Jewish populations.) In particular, there was a robust Jewish community in Mesopotamia in the first centuries of the Common Era, many scholars among them. So there was real contact with Persian religion, and easy traffic back and forth between Mesopotamia and the Land of Israel. Any Jewish law of purities would have been framed in knowledge of the contrasts with the Zoroastrian code of cleanness and uncleanness.

What Neusner tells us is that the Mishnaic and Persian purity codes don't work the same way, and they don't serve the same purposes. For the Zoroastrian system, what is good is clean, and what is evil is unclean. For the Mishnah, by contrast, it very much appears that ultimately, everything is good. Only things can become unclean that have a role in human concerns. The system of purities is not about good and evil, but about shaping human life, sanctifying it and informing it with the spirit of the covenant that grew by stages in history from the Exodus. Quite a transformation: what was in Zoroastrian religion a means of separating life into good and evil, and rejecting the evil as barren, has become in the Mishnah a means of affirming all of life as good, and at the same time a means of sanctifying human life in this good world.

To take only one example, there is a law that appears twice in Exodus and once in Deuteronomy, "thou shalt not seethe a kid in its mother's milk." There are many explanations, but they usually work out to a way of respecting the life in the animals that you have slaughtered for meat, or of respecting the deity that has given you the meat. To understand this a little bit better go to your local county fair, and in the large-animal pens, you will see a cow patiently licking its very young calf into shape. A homely and dowdy example of love among animals, but love it is. And the mother is deeply grieved when you kill the calf for meat. So some kind of respect is appropriate. Virtually all the ancient world treated killing animals for food, especially killing mammals, as occasion for some kind of ritual respect for the life that is taken. That life is treated as a gift, and we ought to be grateful for it. This much comes already from the world-affirming nature religions, but it continues in world-affirming historical religions. What the Mishnah and the Talmuds do is to deepen this sense of respect, and turn it into a way to affirm all of life as a gift. A kosher kitchen does that by keeping meat and dairy products separate from one another.

We have already seen the two groups that survived the destruction of the Temple. The Christians were the first to produce documents. In the New Testament, they followed the model of the inherited scriptures, a mixture of law, history, and covenant. The original history is centered on the Exodus, and the Gospel story is a parody of the Exodus. The Jewish leadership in Palestine had invested high hopes in two revolts, in 67–73 and 132–135 CE. They lost badly the first time, and worse the second. The idea of a messiah was not attractive (twice burned, thrice shy). The Christian scheme of declaring their failed messiah to be a success was hardly attractive. Any attempt to do *another* parody of the Exodus would look like an imitation of the Christians. So the rabbis chose another strategy, and in their different way, they did something very similar to what the Church did. They moved the Temple and its sacrifice into the home and synagogue, where it could not be destroyed again and where it could enrich and sanctify the lives of every Jew everywhere. By studying the new law in the Talmuds, one is effectively performing the Temple sacrifice that can no longer literally be conducted in Jerusalem.

I used to cringe at the phrase in the end of Thomas Aquinas' great Eucharistic hymn, "types and shadows have their ending, for the newer rite is here," thinking it was anti-Jewish. And you could read it in an anti-Jewish way, on the theory that Judaism has been superseded by Christianity (and Christianity has no part in the Judaism of the Second Temple and before; Marcionite theology again!). But in fact the rabbis did the same thing the Church did: the older rite, the Temple sacrifice, was involuntarily ended, by the Romans, and so a replacement was necessary. The rules of kashrut, how to keep a kosher kitchen, and the practice of study of the Torah and Talmud, are the replacements. And they can't be taken away by events of history.

I am presenting in brutally short summary the thesis of Donald Harman Akenson, in *Surpassing Wonder: The Invention of the Bible and The Talmuds*. More than a few scholars have realized that the Church and the Synagogue are both daughters, and both *legitimate* daughters, of Second Temple Judaism. Akenson tells the story with a grandeur that is seldom rivaled.

By stages the Mishnah grew. It attracted two great commentaries, the Talmud of the Land of Israel, known as the Yerushalmi, and the Babylonian Talmud, known as the Bavli. The Yerushalmi was somewhat earlier, more or less complete in the fifth century. The Bavli took a little longer, and in the end, it shaped rabbinic Judaism and gave it the character it has had ever since. Every aspect of life gets some regulation: prayers, domestic housekeeping, marriage, commercial transactions, agriculture, and common worship. How to be a proper Jew, with enchanting tales for the edification of children both young and old along the way.

One might well ask why the Talmuds appeared when they did, especially as they were two to five centuries *after* the Mishnah. The reasons are coming to light at present. When Christianity was established, it was as if the worst fear had come true.

When Christianity became the established religion in the fourth century, under Constantine, many things happened. When there were quarrels among bishops, Constantine summoned the bishops and sat them down together to talk. Constantine endowed a collecting of the texts of the New Testament documents, and a general editing. For there were a lot of variations between different manuscripts. The results were published, in what we know as the "Textus Receptus," the received text. Until the nineteenth century, it was the only text, and not a very good one. (The King James was made from the Textus Receptus.) The recovery of older texts is a story for some other time, not in the present book.

More interesting was the evolving imperial policy that continued to tolerate the Synagogue, but enforced a split between the Church and the Synagogue. Scholars can hear hints of this in the rabbinic documents of the age. It was very much like John Chrysostom, a preacher in Antioch in these years. Chrysostom thought he had a problem. People from his congregation were coming to church on Sunday, but they were also going to Synagogue on Saturday. This doesn't seem like a bad thing to me, but it did to him, and apparently to many others in the fourth century. It is beginning to look as if it was not in the first or even the second century that the parting of the ways was finished, but in the fourth century. It was enforced by Roman law. Boyarin (2004) has much detail.

What followed for the next fourteen or so centuries was the establishment of Christianity. That means more than it appears to in an America that is as secular as it is religious. For us today, religion (meaning Christianity) is a voluntary activity, and everybody knows that, everybody is easy about that. Even when most everybody still goes to church. And in comparison to Europe, America is still a very religious country. But when the Church was established, it was not only not voluntary, not being a Christian was almost unthinkable. That's not a compulsory choice, it's not a choice at all, because it's not *seen*. Jesus is just the way things are; there couldn't be any other way even conceivable.

Except that there was. There are those other people, the stubborn ones, the ones who won't accept Jesus: the Jews. They testify to the choice made in being a Christian, because they don't make it. But even they were a limited witness to choice, because they agreed about three fourths of the Bible, the Common Documents. In the end, what resulted was a way of living together, a way to agree about what we disagree about, a way to have toleration of the Synagogue by the Church, if the Synagogue won't disturb things too much. That was the price to be paid. And the payoff for the Synagogue was that everybody, Jews as well as Christians, got a world that was rock-solid. We can agree about our disagreements, but the Jews won't remind Christians that to participate in biblical religion *at all* is a choice, and one that fends of chaos in the cosmos, existential terror in the face of meaninglessness. We return to relations between Christians and Jews and their root anxieties in section 6.3.

We won't have to face the fact that our religion (either version of it) was an invention of human beings by the actors in and editors of the Pentateuch, the Torah, in the years from the Monarchy through the beginnings of the Second Temple, even if the roots go back to the dim past in the Exodus. We won't have to face the terrible question of Moses at the burning bush: "Who *are* you?" "Do you really mean you want us to leave the comforts of nature for the wilderness of history? Those hard questions were covered up; and covered up, they festered. We next see that embarrassment in section 6.3.

Meaning was safe in the world of the establishment of Christianity, a meaning that didn't have to deal with those hard questions. That world lasted until the French Revolution, when everything came unglued.

5.6 The Menu of Religions in Antiquity

At this point, we have examples of most of the basic kinds of religion. What is new is Gnosticism; that option was not available when the

Exodus religion began, during the Israelite monarchy. Let me list them in functional terms. They are not complicated.

(1) You can say that human life is just part of nature, and your job is to fit into nature naturally. Here, human life in this natural world is affirmed as good. (History may not even be seen in this kind of religion.) This is world-affirming nature religion. Merold Westphal called it "mimetic" religion, because the business of trying to fit into nature naturally gets called "mimesis," or a sort of *imitation* of nature. This is the first form of religion in so-called "primitive" societies virtually everywhere. For modern revivals, see p. 161.

(2) You can say that human life is essentially historical, and then affirm human life in this historical world as good. This is world-affirming historical religion. To make such a religion work, somehow you have to deal with the pains of life positively. And to say that life in this world is good in full view of all the pains that do not get remedied in this life is necessarily to presuppose some sort of transcendence. It may or may not be the kind of transcendence common to Platonism, the philosophy that says there is another world beyond this one, in which you can find spirits, angels, God, ideal forms, and so on. But transcendence of some sort there must be. Your job is to travel through history with that transcendent ultimate reality, trusting that it will take care of you. In plain English, you are traveling through history with a God, one who will take care of you. If life in this world gets affirmed, and nature is part of this world, then nature gets affirmed as good, too; not just history. Merold Westphal called this kind of basic life orientation "historical-covenantal" religion, because it takes life as historical, and the activity of traveling through history in the company of something transcendent is a *covenant*.

(3) You can say that life in this world is defective, your original state was some other (and better) place, and your job is to get back to that better state as fast as you can. Westphal, following Paul Ricoeur, calls this "exilic" religion, because it takes human life in this world as a state of exile from something better and more original. In plain

English, you used to be a disembodied spirit, and you even used to be really part of the divine, part of God. You want to get back to that as soon as possible. Being in a body is a form of imprisonment, escaping from the body is liberation and freedom. This kind of religion gets called "Gnosticism" in the West, but that term usually means the ancient forms of exilic religion. Exilic life orientations can be found unlabeled today.

(4) The Perennial Philosophy: peace of mind and happiness come from meditation, and since meditation can be found in all religions, it is the truth they all share. The Perennial Philosophy is sometimes lumped together with exilic religion, but in a spirit of caution, I'm inclined not to jump to that conclusion.

(5) You can decide that some human institution is the center of value and meaning in human life. Any institution will do: your country, your church, your family, football, the idea of socialism; the list is endless. H. Richard Niebuhr called this "henotheism," because in it you have only one "god." In Greek, *hen* means one. The focus of meaning in life in a henotheism is not really the God of the Bible, and the differences can be subtle. Biblical religion can easily degenerate into a henotheism (and often has). There probably is not a real sense of transcendence here, but I would hesitate to rule it out entirely.

(6) The mystery religions, both ancient and modern. Today we call it "new-age mysticism." Luther Martin (1987) tells the story of the ancient examples.

(7) Lastly, I would name the informal kind of life in the Hellenistic and modern worlds, what just gets called "secularism." Here, people have rituals for dealing with major passages in life, but that is about all. The rituals are vestiges of older religion. There is no theory, and there are no specialists, no experts, because they are unnecessary. You succeed by maximizing pleasure and avoiding pain. (The pains don't bring anything good, so you might as well avoid them.) The rituals bring comfort, perhaps because they are familiar and "traditional."

It is of course possible that Hellenistic and modern secularism could be reduced to the other possibilities, but I'd like to leave that question open. We don't need to answer it. All of these basic religious options are present in the Greco-Roman world, of course, but there was no *theory* of basic religious types such as I am seeking here. Instead, their explanations were pretty "traditional," and that tradition takes a very recognizable shape in Augustine, to whom we come in a moment. Rabbinic Judaism and Christianity were both mixtures of several types. Their common beginning in the Exodus was out of nature religions, and it has sometimes had henotheistic elements to the present day. Exilic religion became a real option only in the Hellenistic world, but the Church and the Synagogue have both been dabbling in it on and off as soon as they were able. These are perennial tendencies in human life, not stages of history that can be passed through and left behind for good.

Still, the story of biblical religion in all its variations has been a story of development from world-affirming nature religion to world-affirming historical religion. The roots of biblical religion were in nature religions of the ancient Near East. The incomplete affirmation of this world as good was extended and completed in historical religion.

Other religions are not as without affirmation of human life in history as they might appear to be. Indian religions *appear* to be cases of exilic religion. That is, in both Hinduism and Buddhism, in some sense, you want to get out of this world of suffering and escape from the cycle of perpetual reincarnations. I emphasize the word "appear" because appearances can be deceptive, and a sense of history and affirmation of human life in this world can show up in surprising places. In Chinese religion, Taoism appears to be a very sophisticated world-affirming nature religion. But the sense of respect for ambiguity found even in the *Tao Te Ching* indicates caution: there may be more here than meets the eye. And the *Tao Te Ching* is soaked in the transformation of yin into yang and back again—and of disappointment into blessing along the way. Confucianism would appear to be a henotheism, in which human life, personal and social, is centered around family and social relationships in traditional China. However that may be, it has held Chinese culture together for thousands of years. It is not obvious what to say about Islam, since it has only one God, and the degree to which Islam fits with world-affirming historical religion is best left for Islamic theologians themselves to consider.

And conversely, there are examples of Christianity that fit all seven types of basic life orientation. The Church often baptized not just new converts but also their old religions, and so world-affirming nature religions live on. The notorious examples are the abuses in which solidarity with the saints is turned into the cult of the saints. There is naturalism (and so functional nature religion) in much of Christian philosophy today.

Functionally exilic religion appears in Christianity from nearly the start all the way to the present. Many Christians think Jesus came to get us out of an evil world, not to save us in a good world. They think human beings are made of discardable bodies and detachable souls. They treasure Platonism even when they've never heard of Plato (they've also not read much of the Bible).

You can certainly find Christians who think salvation comes from the Church, not from God: outside the Church, there is no salvation. (That idea is so traditional that it even has a Latin name, "extra ecclesiam nulla salus.")

The Church functions quite well as a purveyor of Hellenistic-style secular rituals for passages in life. Such folk go to church only for Christmas, Easter, and weddings. (Their funerals are usually not in church.) Sometimes it works better if you *don't* know where the traditions come from. In a non-western culture where Christian-kitsch is popular, I hear that a priest was once told, "You can make a good extra living doing western-style weddings; after all, you already have the costume."

And occasionally, you can actually find Christians who do read the Bible, Common Documents as well as the New Testament, and who do have a sense of the anxieties and frights of history. They actually *relish* those frights. They come back for more. They recognize their anxieties (and thrills) as the fear of the Lord in the Common Documents. We shall see them again in section 7.5.

Chapter 6

From Augustine to the Modern World

6.1 Overview

Perplexed is the best word for the Christian universe today. We are not sure what to make of our own time or our inherited faith, and we are not sure how we got here. This chapter sketches the story, to the minimal extent that it is known. There has been a lot of writing about this history, people don't agree, and much of the story remains to be uncovered.

Before we begin that story, we should look at where we are going in the end. We need more than just how we got here. In the medieval world everything made sense (or we think it did), but in the modern world, Christianity doesn't make sense (though science may). So what are we to do about it today? Partial answers we can find; complete answers probably not.

To put it another way, if in the biblical world the covenant people could see their way through history in the company of the Lord of History, how come we have so much trouble doing that today? The story of the writing of the Bible and its roots in history is not a story of confusion, it was a story of vision and courage—for them; but we are the ones confused.

In chapter 7, we will look at our situation today. In chapter 8 we will look at some of our options today. In the end, though many puzzles will remain unsolved, we shall find ourselves again traveling through history in company with a transcendent Other who doesn't always offer the comfort that we would like. (This, too, is very biblical.) The traditional language is "being *in statu viatoris*," on the way of a pilgrim—but we travel together on a pilgrimage through history, not alone as individuals. In the end, we will return to the exodus from nature into history, but with a new perspective gained from recent scholarship.

We look back with nostalgia on a world that seemed to make sense, and we think the world made coherent sense as late as the nineteenth century, until the time of Darwin. In reality, the breakup began much earlier, in the unraveling of the medieval worldview. The ingredients of an incoherent cosmos were all present by the seventeenth century, long before the nineteenth.

There are a number of studies of the changes on the way to modernity, some classic, some recent. Alexandre Koyré (*From the Closed World to the Infinite Universe*, 1957) and E. A. Burtt (*The Metaphysical Foundations of Modern Physical Science*, 1924) focussed on the changed world of mathematical physics in the seventeenth and eighteenth centuries. Louis Dupré's *Passage to Modernity* (1993) surveys cultural changes of a much wider scope. Dupré's account tells so much that is unfamiliar that it would be foolhardy to think we understand our own time or the roads to it at all well. John Courtney Murray's *The Problem of God* (1964), briefly guides his readers through the differences between the medieval and post-modern worlds. Our own time, the "post-modern" world, bears surprising parallels with the biblical world, unlike the medieval or modern worlds. That should offer some comfort. C. S. Lewis's *The Discarded Image* (1964) offers something that few have time for: a taste of the cultural riches that were lost on the way to the modern world. As Dupré tells it, the high middle ages had a sort of cosmic synthesis, in which God, man, and world all fit together. It was replaced not by a sense of living in history (which is what we need now) but by disconnection between man and the world and between both and God. Relationships between them have been lost. Nature (or the world) had a natural presence of God in its workings. Today, the nature we know from the sciences has no meaning in it at all.

To put it a little differently, we used to live in a cosmos in which everything made sense, everything had a place, and everything had a relationship to everything else. We have come from a cosmos to a horizon, a world in which we can see only so far, the horizon moves with us, and we are a people on a journey, whether or not any want to call it a pilgrimage. That is the color of post-modernity. To get a little ahead of our story, we have become complainers, doubters, skeptics, demanding the comforts that were last available in the medieval world, threatening to look for some other basic life orientation if we don't get those comforts again. In between, in the modern world, things still fitted together—in a manner of speaking, mostly scientific speaking. And in such a world, much that matters to human beings is left out.

The medieval cosmos had both the joys and the hazards of a coherent system, or at least we think it did, in our anxiety that seeks a time to be nostalgic about. The joys: the world feels safe and familiar. The hazards: progress is blocked, because any change would destabilize the system. In reality, the medieval world was a synthesis, not a system: it was put together out of parts that came from diverse places, parts that did not all fit together as comfortably as they appear to have in hindsight. When such a system is defended against destabilizing forces, it can become bad faith: that is, defenders try to make it appear necessary, when in fact it was a human construction, and somewhat miscellaneous.

The outcome is that science and history stand out today, and most people see only science. Historical thinking is not trusted, or not seen at all. Globalization has made religious plurality a fact of life, and other religions are a live option in America today. What is more, we are not comfortable with having our religion exposed as a human construction—after all, how can it be God's work if it is also a human construction? If it is a human construction, it looks as if we are betrayed into nihilistic relativism. That is to get ahead of our story, but we can at least say, in forecast, that the major challenges to biblical religion today come from history, relativity, and pluralism. The major challenge *appears* to come from science, but I shall argue that appearance is highly misleading. In the meantime, we need to look at a little of how we got to where we are today.

6.2 A Bishop in North Africa

In the end of the fourth century and beginning of the fifth of the common era, the region of North Africa that is now Tunisia was not the center of the Empire, but it was also not so rural as to be marginal. The local big city was Carthage, and somewhat to the west of it was a seaport town called Hippo, in what is now Algeria. It was big enough for its Christians to have their own bishop. From about 395 to about 430, when he died, Augustine, sometime playboy and stand-up philosopher, was the local bishop. There were people to teach, babies to baptize, priests to train, parishes and monasteries to oversee, preaching all the time, and always questions to answer. And he wrote. He wrote a lot; in collections from the period, he is rivaled only by John Chrysostom in the East and by nobody in the West. He was somewhat disorderly in his thinking, by later standards, but the richness of his thought makes up some for the disorder. He summed up an age and set the problems for everybody who came after him.

The Roman Empire was beginning to show signs of weakness, but it had presided over many centuries of a common civilization, common trade, culture, and to some extent, of peace. That was ending. The "barbarians" would sack Rome for the first time in these years (410

CE). The old Roman gods, shared with the Greeks and every right-thinking individual, had lost a lot of credibility; and not everybody was right-thinking anymore. In fact, the troublemakers (i. e., Christians) had infiltrated some of the highest places in the government.

As often happens in such a time of impending crisis, those who saw their interests coinciding with the establishment tried to prop up that establishment as long as possible. And they naturally disliked any who appeared to weaken the establishment. When the barbarians sacked Rome, the learned pagans blamed the Christians. (With some reason, because these barbarians *were* Christians, if of the Arian variety.) This kind of talk was in the air, everywhere; in North Africa in particular. And so Augustine the bishop of Hippo had to deal with it. He wrote.

I choose Augustine to sum up a long and complicated history of the first centuries of Christian life, because you can find most of the ideas that were passed on to later centuries in his book, *The City of God Against the Pagans*. Christianity had become common enough that the remaining pagans were feeling threatened, and they mounted considerable arguments against the new religion. Augustine's book was designed to counter those arguments. In doing so, he summed up what Christians were doing, what they believed, and how they saw the cosmos. It is not an account of world-affirming historical religion as this book describes it. Augustine's language is much more familiar than is mine. But the parts of a world-affirming historical religion are all there, quite recognizable in *The City of God*.

The pagan philosophers complained about the pains of life; they wanted (some of the time) to affirm life in this world, and (some of the time) to avoid or escape the pains of life in this world. Not consistent, but who would notice? For them, life in this world is broken and defective because of its pains. Clearly, the pains bring no blessing. They are barren.

People complain that good and evil events fall on good and evil people indiscriminately—but why? In answer, Augustine did not say what I would say—the pains each bear their own blessings, namely, freedom, creativity, and fellowship (cf. p. 6 above). He said that for the wicked, the pains are deserved punishment, and for the good, the pains are an opportunity to learn. The painful parts of life are still, in and of themselves, not yet wholly good. Better would be to say they have not yet been wholly integrated into a life that is good. For then, as now, the pains of life are good because they are part of life, not because they are painful. A hard distinction when life hurts, especially since we rightly pray that the pains will go away.

Augustine did not think that evil is a thing existing in itself, but instead a lack of goods that should be there, a *privation*, in his language. This is a part of life that will always cause trouble. For if the pains hurt (and how they do!), and if they can sometimes rightly be avoided (we pray to God to make the pains go away, as we should), then no matter how we speak of the pains of life, it will always be possible to interpret our language as writing them off as barren. Even Jesus asked to have the pains go away, when he saw what was about to happen to him. Language will always be ambiguous, and never more so than when people try to find good in the pains of life. Still, where Augustine's opponents wrote the pains off as the work of fate, fortune, or evil demons, and saw the gods as their ticket of escape from the pains, Augustine clearly wants something more constructive, more life-affirming.

It has been easy to subvert Augustine, by reading him selectively, or by leaving out parts of his argument. He looked forward to a resurrected life in heaven, in a physical body, against the Gnostics. He can be read to make heaven not the transformation and perfecting of this life on earth, but instead as a better place, a place of escape from this life on earth. (It is hard *not* to read the later parts of *City of God* this way.) Soon readers let the "body" part of life in heaven be shadowed, if not denied, and the immortal soul takes over in its place. Then we have some of the comforts of Gnosticism, sold under Christian trademarks and without the bitter anti-worldly edge of the Gnostic original. That idea creeps over readers insidiously, unnoticed.

Augustine also laid the groundwork for many confusions in later centuries; natural confusions, some of them even innocent. He took miracles in the New Testament as proofs of its message, instead of as advertisements like those we know on TV today. In fairness, people in his time and centuries afterward often treated unexplained medical recoveries as miracles. But to think one can reason *from* miracles and fulfilled prophecies *to* the truth of Christianity is a grave mistake. One cannot reason to a starting point, only from it; and so the Christianity that was supposed to be an act of faith becomes the consequence of faith in something else. One surreptitiously comes to believe not in the goodness of life in full view of its pains but in escape from those pains, for that is what a literal reading of the miracle texts inevitably fosters. Augustine is merely typical; sometime before him, readers took the miracles as selling escape from the limitations of life, not a way to live with them and find blessing in them. That way of reading the New Testament texts has made enormous trouble in recent centuries.

On the other side, sometimes he offered good advice for how to avoid confusion, advice that was often ignored. In the *Handbook on Christian Doctrine*, he told readers that when the literal meaning of the text is unbelievable or uncharitable, they should give it up and find some other meaning. A literal reading of scripture in later years has grown out of assumptions that were widespread in the first centuries of the Common Era, and it became more literal rather than less as the years rolled on. How much trouble in the last three centuries would have been avoided if Augustine's advice had been heeded!

Sometimes he saw far more than he knew. His ideas about life in time in the *Confessions* were fifteen centuries ahead of his time; philosophers finally caught up with him only in the twentieth century. His instinct that God lives *outside* of time would have saved an enormous amount of theological confusion, some of it quite mischievous. It is still too often ignored.

Augustine's concept of action has caused a lot of trouble since his time. It was innocent enough in his own time; it was only the changing later context that turned his ideas into a source of trouble. There is a window in *The City of God* into the ideas that will grow and change over time, leading us to our own confusions in the modern world. It is in Book 5, chapter 9 (pp. 201–202 of the Dyson translation):

> Moreover, even if a certain order of causes does exist in the mind of God it does not follow that nothing is left to the free choice of our will. For our wills are themselves included in the order of causes which is certain to God and contained within His foreknowledge. For the wills of men are the causes of the deeds of men, and so He Who has foreseen the causes of all things clearly cannot have been ignorant of our wills among those causes, since he foresaw them to be the causes of our deeds.

So far, so good. Augustine does not distinguish between the many senses of "efficient cause," as we shall see below on p. 128. For now, continue with Augustine:

> Moreover, when Cicero admits [translator's footnote: *De fato*, 10, 20f] that nothing happens unless preceded by an efficient cause, this is in itself sufficient to rebut what he says in this matter. He says that nothing happens without a cause, but that not every cause is determined by fate, because there is also a fortuitous cause, a natural cause, and a voluntary cause.

Cicero evidently knew that there are many kinds of efficient cause, including what is simply natural (a misleadingly simple term for us), and what is random, i. e., inexplicable. Augustine will force them all together, because he is interested only in one. He continues:

> But how does this help him? It is enough that he confesses that nothing happens unless preceded by a cause. As to

> those causes which he calls fortuitous, from which the word 'fortune' is also derived: we do not say that these do not exist, but that they are hidden, and we attribute them to the will of the true God, or to that of spirits of some kind or another.

Augustine fudges here: he admits that chance is real, but assigns it (he docs not say how) to the will of God.

> Furthermore, we do not by any means separate even natural causes from the will of Him Who is the Author and Creator of all nature.

Here he does the same thing with natural causes.

> Finally, voluntary causes belong either to the will of God or to that of angels or men or certain animals (if, that is, we may apply the term 'will' to those movements of the non-rational animals by which they act according to their nature when they seek or shun something). When I speak of the wills of angels, I mean both the good angels, whom we call angels of God, and the wicked angels, whom we call angels of the devil, or also demons; and, by the same token, I mean both good and bad men.
>
> From this discussion, then, we reach the conclusion that all things which come to pass have no efficient causes which are not voluntary causes: belonging, that is, to that Nature which is the Breath of life.

Augustine pushes all the senses of efficient causation together, making it easier for later generations to think there is only one kind of efficient cause, and that is *will*, intentional will that simply directs the motions of bodies. Natural causes were a category that meant something quite different for Augustine (and as late as the middle ages) than they do for us. For the ancient and medieval world, nature, as in human nature, was animate, where for us, natural causes are precisely what is *not* animate, even in living things. For the medievals, nature was the principle of self-originating motion in all living things. Indeed, rocks and the weather were conceived the same way that animals were: they move, of their own accord, where we would just assign the motions to gravity and climate dynamics. The four elements likewise all move on their own, from principles contained within each one. Air (wind), fire (rising in air), and water (rivers, tides, waves), are all obvious. But earth motion also (earthquakes; cf. Psalm 114) was well-known to the ancients. (They would have been giddy with delight if they had known about plate tectonics!) We reduce the self-originated motions of animals (including humans) to natural causes that have nothing to do with will or intention or purpose. In the process, we have lost the ability to relate nature to will, intention, purpose, and meaning in life. How that happened will take a little telling.

Why did Augustine push all the senses of efficient cause together? Because he wanted to hold humans responsible for their actions, and because he wanted to point to the providence of God in all things. It is as if the hearer of the flood joke (p. 3 above), challenged to defend the action of God in the rescues that were declined, insists that God somehow *physically* affected the intentions of the rescuers in the two pickup trucks, the boat, and the helicopter.

Psychology and philosophy are still working to extricate themselves from the idea that the human will is a physical cause. We saw some of the poisonous fruit of this idea in regard to divine actions in *Waters*, and again in *Where, Now, O Biologists*.

Another problem bears mention. Most Christians believed the Church had displaced Judaism in God's affections. Augustine was not an exception. For the present, Jews are not to be killed, but ultimately, rabbinic Judaism is supposed to go out of business. Augustine, though no friend of rabbinic Judaism, may nevertheless have been a voice for protecting it from the worst violence, simply because he wanted Jews to survive as witnesses (against their will) to the validity of New

Testament claims and Old Testament prophecies. If supersessionism with toleration had been the worst of anti-Jewish theology, it would have been bad enough, but not homicidal. It was not the worst, as is well known.

These parts of Augustine's theology are only being corrected in the present. For the centuries that followed, it would be fair to say that Augustine was the teacher. He was *the* theologian and philosopher until the middle ages, and in many ways even into the present. The road from Augustine to Descartes is long, and we have time only for a few events that bear on our own story, on how present-day biblical religion became so confused.

First let me take an important detour. Most of our story is about philosophy, because most of the confusions today are philosophical. But not all. Some of them are about religious quarrels, and the deepest and longest lasting quarrel has been between Christians and Jews.

6.3 The Skeleton in the Closet

Relations between the Church and the Synagogue were not particularly friendly during the first millennium of their common life together, but Christians and Jews were not always at each other's throats, either. Bad as it was, the level of violence was low compared to what came afterward. More serious trouble started with the First Crusade.

What comes as a surprise is that relations between Christians and Jews until the ninth or tenth century were not worse. Indeed, Judaism was attractive to Christians, and laws were necessary to prevent Christians from converting to Judaism. In the fourth century, when John Chrysostom was preaching in Antioch, Judaism was even more attractive. Chrysostom states with embarrassing clarity the root of the problem between the Church and the Synagogue: in effect, the implication of his words is that we can't both be right. We have seen Chrysostom already in section 5.5; We shall see these themes again in section 7.2. But Chrysostom's words were like modern political cartoons—understood in their own time as outrageous exaggeration. In later centuries, read at face value, they were incitement to outrageous atrocities.

The idea that "we can't both be right" is the claim that only one daughter religion can legitimately inherit from Second Temple Judaism. Think of it as the Great Exclusive Or. We saw pluralism in the roots of the Bible, in the tribes that came together in and after the Exodus. The Great Exclusive Or is a repudiation of pluralism. Pluralism, of course, comes at a cost: you have to take responsibility for your own tradition, you have to admit your own role in continuing your own tradition, you have to admit your forefathers' role in inventing your own tradition, because there is another tradition next-door growing out of the same roots, another way to carry on the Exodus covenant. In a word, one has to face the anxieties of history.

The alternative rises to view in the Epistle of Barnabas, only to be denounced. "Take heed now to yourselves, and not to be like some, adding largely to your sins, and saying, 'The covenant is both theirs and ours.' " (The text is in *The Ante-Nicene Fathers*, vol. 1, ed. Roberts and Donaldson, p. 138; *Barnabas*, ch. 4) The covenant is both theirs and ours: what a possibility! It would mean a responsible liberty of interpretation in the conduct of a covenant.

In the New Testament, John (and before it, Matthew) are one side of a messy quarrel, the other side is not well recorded in the rabbinic literature, although there are hints. Mark and Luke-Acts have far less serious problems. In Paul, Galatians is directed to Judaizers rather than to Jews, and Romans 9–11, while not calculated to make non-Christian Jews feel good about themselves, clearly thinks the covenant is still valid for all of Judaism. It could have served well as an upper bound on Christian anti-Judaism, had there been will to use it as that. Instead, it was more like a lower bound.

The Gospels and Paul are about quarrels *between* Jews, for the first Christian writers were all Jews. These texts have been re-read later as quarrels *against* Jews. That can be corrected.

Return to the events in the middle ages, and from them to the modern world. In 1095, the first Crusade was proclaimed against the "infidels," and the mobs that set out for the Holy Land decided to clean house at home first. Relations between Jews and Christians had evidently worsened some in the ninth and tenth centuries, and so violent anti-semitism was possible as it had not been before. Jews were murdered by the hundreds in Germany and France. Pogroms followed, Jews were driven from one European country to another, and there has been sporadic violence more or less continuously until the twentieth century. The Enlightenment tried to integrate Jews into a secularizing culture, and when that didn't work (faithful Jews didn't cooperate), the response in the nineteenth and twentieth centuries was to eliminate them. Again.

Why put this sordid history in the middle of a tale of how basic religious concepts grew? If the basic religious history is the foreground, relations between Christians and Jews are the background. Relations between the two surviving Exodus traditions have distorted the conceptual development of philosophy and theology. In a word, if one's own community is engaged in denial of the exposure that comes from the mere existence of the other Exodus tradition, that denial, like a sore tooth or a sour stomach, will color how one sees the world.

We saw in contrast to radical monotheism of the later biblical traditions the possibilities for henotheisms and gnosticisms and the nature religions out of which biblical religion grew. Biblical religion can also degenerate back into those possibilities, and it can do so covertly, surreptitiously, and insidiously. It is tempting to try to get out of the responsibility of interpretation and the anxieties of history that come with it. The temptation offers the comforts of a One True Faith, from which the we-people can look out on the world on the they-people and watch the they-people being wasted. The outsiders are no longer a threat, and you don't have to take them into account when you make sense of the world or your tradition. It's OK to fight them. With openness to another tradition comes openness of other kinds, in particular, openness to the world as it can be seen from new eyes. But when the mind is closed to other traditions, one can fit the world to one's own desires.

6.4 Night Flight to Modernity

The thirteenth century was a time of philosophical challenge and response. Thomas Aquinas is typical of his age, and noteworthy for many reasons. For us, it is enough to say that in his century and the next (he died in 1274), Christian philosophers were re-integrating this world and the human with transcendence, the divine. Their work has shaped the seven centuries since in a profound way. The 1300s were a time of philosophical crisis, if such a thing can seem possible today. In the time from Augustine to Aquinas, Christian philosophy had largely built on Augustine, and that meant on a Christianized Plato and on the Bible. Augustine's instincts for interpreting the Bible were not to be challenged seriously until the nineteenth century. But in the thirteenth, relations between theology and philosophy were shaken to their roots. Much of Aristotle's philosophy was unavailable in the West until the thirteenth century. Translations of previously unknown works of Aristotle came to Europe for the first time then.

Plato and Platonism had seemed congenial to Christian thought from nearly time immemorial. Platonism makes things seem simple and comfortable. And Platonism made it easy for a thinker to get to God, because God appears directly in all the explanations of the world. We saw this with Augustine's explanation of all motion as will-directed motion on p. 113 above.

Aristotle was different. God was absent, and the point is to look at the world for its own sake. Where Plato had left the doors open for the divine at every turn, Aristotle was interested in a world that could be known on its own terms, without recourse to anything transcendent at all. Aristotle was also averse to mathematics. Mathematics has usually traveled with Platonism. When Aristotelians have been ascendent over Platonists, mathematics has suffered. Aristotle's world was without creation, ruled by a determinism of sorts, leaving no room for a provident God. Man was a creature of matter, and like it, subject to corruption. Moral perfection did not involve God.

As M.-D. Chenu, a twentieth-century Dominican, put it, "The face of Aristotle's philosophy was turned earthward." Assimilating Aristotle would take a very careful—and creative—reading. That is what Thomas did. He synthesized the confessional philosophy and theology of Augustine and the Platonists with the critical thought of Aristotle. We would do better to take Thomas as a role model than simply to repeat his philosophical theology: Biblical religion faces new ideas from time to time, and the challenges come in the form of critical thought. The response I am peddling is one in which the confessional tradition once again gets synthesized with the new critical thought. For in our own time, we face a new critical challenge, and it comes not from Aristotle, not even from the natural sciences, but from the historical thinking that grew up in the nineteenth century. Like Aristotle, it has its face turned earthward, and the comfortable paths to God in nineteenth century "orthodoxy" don't fare too well under the light of criticism.

The changes that started with the assimilation of Aristotle are not a story I could tell, even if there were space here. Those who can tell the story sound like travellers returned from a strange and distant land, full of fabulous and wonderful beasts, strange beliefs in the middle ages and the ancient world. Suffice it to say that the synthesis of God, man, and nature that Augustine first put together out of Platonist materials and Aquinas rebuilt with Aristotelian parts fell apart in the few centuries after Aquinas. As much could have been expected from the way I have told the story of Augustine's account of will and motion, p. 113 above. He put together things that for us today don't seem to belong together at all.

There were other changes in the thirteenth and fourteenth centuries. People started thinking about the relation between faith and reason as they had not ever before. The reasoning voice of faith asked itself how it knew God. Such exercises can be taken in more than one way. If you read them as a believing soul asking itself why it believes in God, they don't do much damage, and they may even help some. But if you read them as strict proofs intended to underwrite faith or logically to force non-believers to believe, they are disasters. In the centuries since, the alleged "proofs" have all been shot down. Those who relied upon them for their faith were then left without support. But faith should not rest on proofs; it just is, as we saw in *Unwelcome Good News*. Either you do look for blessings in all of life, pains included, or you don't. You take history seriously, or you don't. It's a choice. But it did not seem that way in the later Middle Ages; for them, at least some of the time, the right choice could be proven.

That was not what we saw in *Unwelcome Good News*. There, you will be compared with other people, some who rejected exposure, limitation, and need, and others who embraced them at great cost to themselves, confident that these pains of life bring blessings, whether visible or invisible. It is possible to compare people's lives and ask, "Whom do you want to be like?" You can see quite enough of what you are choosing from, but it is not something that could be proven.

People rarely come to (or remain in) Christian faith because of a chain of reasoning. Usually, it is because of events of grace in the life of the believer, on the basis of which (in his or her experience, at least) he *has* to believe; not to would be irrational or ungrateful. If not events, it can be just longing for grace. Or he sees others who have had experiences of grace and says, "I want what they have." Philosophy just gets in the way, at least at the beginning.

Such faith is more like the starting point for proof than its end. Aquinas knew this very well, for he says as much in the *Summa*, Part I, Question 1, article 8. But his instinct was subverted and then forgotten. The famous Five Ways in the second Question of the *Summa* are today often taken as reason's access to God, without resort to revelation.

6.5 The World Through Graph-Paper Glasses

Between Aquinas and Descartes, there were great changes in the life of Europe. The Reformers came, and left the Church in apparent shambles, fractured in a way that was not just a scandal but seemed the end of the world. Blood was shed, and shed in vain, to put it back together. The hatreds last in some places to the present day. By 1650, after the Thirty Years War, Europe was exhausted. Religious claims to absoluteness were looking a little tarnished by mid-century. That did not stop people from arguing.

But what the 1600s are really famous for is probably Galileo Galilei and Isaac Newton, and among philosophers, René Descartes. Look at the new science first. Galileo reconceived the philosophy of nature that he inherited. Augustine's and Aquinas's synthesis of this world and the divine was ripe to come apart, and in the Aristotelian instinct, this world could and should be studied apart from God. What was new was bringing mathematics (a Platonist love) to the Aristotelian curiosity about this world in its own right.

There is a verse in the Wisdom of Solomon that Augustine quoted over and over again in his commentary *On the Literal Meaning of Genesis*: "O God, thou hast numbered and measured and weighed all things." As I worked through that commentary, finally, in exasperation, I said to myself, "But *you*, O Augustine, wouldn't number or measure or weigh anything, not anything at all!" Strictly speaking, I was being a bit unfair; there is a little arithmetic in *The City of God*, but not much.

Galileo started to measure, to weigh, and to count. Aristotle said that physics is the study of things that change in time. This has continued to the present, despite many scientists' ingratitude to Aristotle. What was new in the 1600s was studying change with mathematics. Galileo started to measure, but it was Descartes who brought system to the new vision of the world. It is as if Descartes laid down a thin film of graph paper on the whole world. Physicists see everything through glasses that have little squares drawn all over them.

And through those glasses with little squares on them, the whole world looks different. That was the most visible change in the seventeenth century, and it is not easy to see how big a change it was. For now, whenever anything moves, it has a path (a "trajectory") that is defined down to the level of indivisible points. It can be calculated, it can be photographed, it can be measured. And it follows rules.

Such rules came to be known as laws of nature. The model was the planets in the night sky, and when Newton's work was done, people knew where the planets were to the smallest fraction of a degree. If you look at a cyclist on the road in front of you, about a half mile away, his head takes up an angle about an arc-minute wide. An arc-minute is a sixtieth of a degree. Astronomers today know planetary positions to a thousandth of an arc-*second*, a sixtieth of a minute. (Actually, they know where Mars is to within a few centimeters, because they can measure its position with lasers!)

It was a new world. In the world of Aristotelian science, the model was life, organisms (Aristotle was a biologist, after all), and a rock in the air falls because it wants to go home, to its natural resting place. After Galileo and Descartes and Newton, rocks are inanimate, but they obey natural laws, like parts of a machine. It was as if God had set up the universe like giant clockwork. As the hands and gears of a clock turn round and round, the planets turn round and round. As hammers and ratchets in a clock push on one another, in the same way, moving objects in ordinary life push on each other. It is all very predictable. We call the new way of looking at the world empirical science.

What happened next is, I suppose, to be expected when people take analogies literally. Since God made the machine that is the world, one could look at the world and figure out the mind of God. Except that if there's no place in the machine for the operator to interact with it (and soon there was not), one could also say that the machine just *is*. Then you can get along just fine without God at all. Perhaps sensing the danger, Robert Boyle, physicist and leading English scientist, endowed a series of annual lectures, devoted to the task of proving that God exists. No one would ever have doubted the existence of God had not people tried to prove it. The result was one more crack in the separation of God from the world.

The proofs of the existence of God didn't work. They never do. What people focused on were miracles, the fantastic stories in the Bible, especially the New Testament, where God (usually meaning Jesus) apparently breaks the rules of nature. But those rules in the 1600s were different from what they had been before. In the 1600s, deviation from the rules could be measured, and so you could put a number on how well or badly a falling rock obeyed the rules. Before that time, rules were flexible things, and to say that a rule was broken was a matter of judgement. After that time, it would look *extremely* odd if you ever saw a rule broken. Room for judgement was gone.

For example, in Joshua 10:13, the sun stands still in the sky for almost a day during a battle. Before modern physics, it was quite believable for the sun to stand still, even if it had never happened before or since. After mathematical astronomy and the physics that came with it, it is very hard to believe such a story. In a contest between God and laws of nature, in the mind of the eighteenth century, God loses. Faith in God became faith in the unchangeableness of the laws of motion of physical bodies. Where beforehand, it was God that made the world a safe and secure place, now, it is the laws of nature that make the world a safe and secure place. The older faith responded (and still responds today) that the God who made the laws of nature can make exceptions to them. The problem with allowing violations of law is that once you do, you can no longer use the law as a tool in deciding what's possible and what's not. Without laws of nature, the world has no order at all. Prediction becomes impossible.

The character of nature has changed quietly. Before, in Aristotelian physics, things in the natural world had "natures," they moved according to their given natures, and according to the purposes in their natures. This was not the world of the nature religions, in which natural motion was personal motion, and a shaman could talk to the animals or the weather; Aristotle's world lay in between that world and our world. In the modern world, for a natural object to have a "nature" is merely for it to obey natural laws. You can't talk to rocks, nor do they have purposes built into their motions. Inanimate objects are more radically inanimate than they ever were before. The groundwork was laid for Darwin two hundred years later, when even plants and animals were stripped of what internal purpose they had left.

More has happened unnoticed than just looking at the world through graph-paper glasses. The stories in the Bible get read literally, but the meaning of "literally" has been changed by the experience of the new science. Edward Hobbs saw that the miracles in the Gospels make better sense as TV advertisements than as "literal" stories. But when you look at those stories through graph-paper glasses, what you see is nothing like TV advertisements. It's more like the movies. TV advertisements pull your leg all the time, but the movies would *never* pull your leg.

This was not just the end of miracles. The end of one thing was the beginning of another, and more interesting is what happened next. Once people looked at the world through graph-paper glasses, they started to read biblical texts more carefully. The texts in the Bible became factual accounts of the past, literally true. And factual accounts can be questioned in ways that a loving father's comforting stories cannot. The spirit of listening to them is quite different. The criticism that was first directed at the Bible was later directed at history; that story we come to in later chapters.

The seventeenth and eighteenth centuries transformed the view of both the world and human knowledge. A medieval dispute about whether we know the things we see with or without actively interpreting them was reopened. Philosophers, David Hume most notably, tried to conceive human knowledge of the world as being without active human interpretation. Everything in the mind was first in the senses. What comes in through the eyes and ears gets sorted out by association, without much processing at all. One doesn't have to know what "red" means to know that that structure over there is red, and it doesn't take interpretation to tell whether it is a house or a barn. For much of modern philosophy, in the beginning was Hume. It didn't work very well, and Immanuel Kant started the long road back to understanding human understanding as a process of active interpretation.

It was that way with interpretation of the Bible, too, for at least some. John Locke is the parallel to David Hume: He let people read the Bible without any help from experts, because the text interprets itself, and the literal meaning is obvious to any sensible man. He wanted to get rid of all supervision by priests, government, and any other official busy-bodies, so that merchants and entrepreneurs could make money more efficiently. There was a social motive, one of individualism. David Laird Dungan tells the story well in his *A History of the Synoptic Problem* (1999). Here lies one of the roots of modern biblical literalism. Later, the idea that the Bible is self-interpreting also did not work, and modern biblical scholarship was born. That is ahead of our story, but the preliminaries for it were laid here, in the seventeenth and eighteenth centuries.

Many today take René Descartes as the beginning of serious philosophy. (For scientists, it would be Newton or Galileo, but that's not much different.) In a graph-paper world, *things* in the world take up space, they have a place in the graph paper. But *thinking* does not. And so mind and body become different kinds of entities, and Descartes has to find a connection between them. Otherwise, the mind will not be able to control the body. This is one example of the growing separation of man from world that has plagued philosophy since the fourteenth century.

Body and soul (here mind) have become separated for Descartes. At this point, one can go two ways, depending on individual preference. If you want to get rid of souls, God, and an "other" world entirely, that way is open and easy to take: The world of matter, what you can see through graph-paper glasses, is self-sufficient, and doesn't need

God at all. It is just nature, and this nature is a modern nature, unlike the ancient and medieval nature, for here, self-originated motion is mechanical and not animate. It has nothing to do with any built-in purposes. It doesn't need external purposes either, because natural motion has now become exhaustively deterministic. Once the world is started, it just goes on forever in its natural way.

If, on the other hand, you want to keep human concerns such as souls and God, there is a problem, the problem of how to re-connect what Descartes put asunder (actually it happened before Descartes, on Louis Dupré's account). How can souls influence bodies, how can humans have free wills, how can will be effective in the physical world? This was the problem that Augustine dodged, as we saw on p. 113 above.

The Enlightenment of the eighteenth century started down the first path, the way of nature without God. It saw itself as a time of liberation from the authority of the Church and the weight of history. Some wanted a self-conscious revival of the ancient Greek and Roman religions. They would not have called their project a "world-affirming nature religion," but that's what it was. For they wanted to affirm life in this world, against the cautions and chastened sobriety of the Church, and they wanted to affirm life in this world *as nature*, without the burden of history. It was nature as newly known by the sciences, and so it was a new naturalism, not in every respect like the ancient naturalisms or the aboriginal shamanistic nature religions. But it was a nature religion nonetheless. And even if it was promoted by only a few (most remained faithful to the Church or the Synagogue, after all), those few had a disproportionate influence in the years to come.

6.6 The New Supernatural

How does one solve Descartes' problem, the problem of reconnecting mind and body, will and willed motions? The instinctive move for believers was just to follow the traditional notion that will is a mover of things in the world and interpret it in terms of the new physics: In the seventeenth century, the language of will-directed motion became the language of a physical cause. In a human action, the human will is the cause of the motions of the act. In an act of God, the divine will is the cause of divinely willed motions in this world. In *Where, Now* I called will-directed motion *volokinesis*, a convenient term for the concept of will as a physical cause. *Volo-* means will, and *-kinesis* means motion.

Forgotten were the other meanings of efficient cause, which we noted but did not give details of in commenting on Augustine above, p. 113, when we saw Augustine lay out the assumption that has now, in the seventeenth century, become will as a physical cause. Here are some other meanings of efficient cause. They come from Collingwood (1940, chapters 29–34), with some modifications: In engineering, the cause of a car crash depends on who could have averted it: the driver, the bartender, the mother of the driver, the civil engineer, the automotive engineer. The cause is whatever could have been done (but was not) to prevent the accident. In physics (today, for us), the cause is whatever makes sense of the sequence of physical motions. It is a question of mathematics. In history, the cause of one person's actions was other people's actions that gave him a motive. Only in physics does the cause ever determine the effects; engineering and history are quite different. And that is not to speak of acts of God at all.

Action has been re-conceived in the terms of the new science. To make something happen, there has to be a physical cause, and so action (or the willing part of action, its intentional component) has to become a physical cause. In acts of God, what was before merely the unusual (but in human terms, gracious) has now become an exception to a law of nature, because that is the only way for anything to be unusual. After laws of nature, everything is predictable and orderly in nature, and nothing would be unusual except a violation of a law of nature.

This is a subtle and surreptitious but also profound change from the older way of thinking about acts of God. In the older way, acts of God worthy of note were deviations from what was expected to happen. Human expectations, however, are not rigid, are often mistaken, and only tell how things *usually* happen. They merely express familiarity with the world and how the world works, both naturally and socially. And things often deviate from the usual. What makes an event miraculous, in the older way of thinking, was not so much its unusualness as its graciousness. It offered opportunities for life, "life more abundantly," when none were expected. Graciousness is about human involvements in the world, purposes, meaning, life and death, human risk, human rewards, life more abundantly. None of that is at all visible to the natural sciences.

Look a little closer at the system of nature into which acts of God have been fitted in the seventeenth century. Nature is composed of bodies that move according to mathematical laws. The only way for something to be unusual would be to deviate from the pertinent mathematical law of motion. And so deviation from a law of motion becomes the criterion that defines and constitutes an act of God *as* an act of God. Graciousness in the lives of human beings has been forgotten, made as invisible to philosophy as it is to the sciences. On the testimony of Louis Dupré (*Passage to Modernity*), the separation of nature and grace was a change prepared long before the 1600s, and merely given mathematical form in that century. Be that as it may (his story is complicated, and I do not entirely understand it), the problems of the seventeenth century can to some extent be understood without their preparation.

To re-conceive acts of God as violations of laws of nature is to think of acts of God in thoroughly naturalistic terms. It is a new naturalism, to be sure, different from the natural world of the ancient shamanisms, the nature religions that were aboriginal everywhere. But naturalism it is. It is commonly known as the "supernatural," to mark the deviations from the modern natural laws that it depends on. The modern supernatural is not really like the medieval supernatural. Among Thomists, the supernatural is usually what Lutherans just call "grace." By contrast, the modern supernatural is a super sort of naturalism, a naturalism by other means. Grace is separate, added on later, by human beings for human purposes, but the thing itself is all about deviations from laws of nature.

There is a problem, of course, with this way of thinking about acts of God (and human acts, too, for that matter). You can *try* to define an act of God as an exception to a law of nature. But laws of nature do not *have* exceptions. If they do, they are not really laws of nature. The way around that was to say that since God made the laws of nature, he can suspend them at will. This does not solve the problem, though for some, it appears to, even today. For if laws of nature have exceptions, there really is no scientific way to tell *when* you are looking at an exception, and then there is no way to tell how as-yet not understood natural phenomena might be obeying some law of nature still to be discovered. Science becomes impossible. The solution to *this* problem has been very simple: People have no trouble telling when they are doing science (and the world is orderly) and when they are thinking about providence (and natural laws have exceptions). They hid the exceptions in places where they cannot be verified or disproven by science, and it is silently assumed that these places give God enough room to do whatever he wants with events in the world. It's a way of thinking that is remarkably hard to catch red-handed. It is not spelled out, of course, because to do that would give the game away: Two ways of speaking about events have been confused with one another, in order to give an appearance of objectivity to acts of God.

If there were problems with divine action, the problems with human action were no less. When volokinesis is taken as the model for action, it reduces action to changes of state in two systems—mind and world, with a physical cause connecting them. It doesn't see all the things in the background world that make an act be an act.

There appear to be only two choices at this point. One can take will as real and non-natural in the sense of being outside of nature but working like nature, since it supplies physical causes to make acts happen. The problems with this choice are the same as those with divine action as supernatural.

The other choice is to abolish will entirely, since there is no interfering with natural motions. Action is then just something attributed to physical motions after the fact, and those physical motions are pre-determined anyway. (As it happens, they are not pre-determined; quantum indeterminacy will give you that much, but the seventeenth and eighteenth centuries didn't know that.) In any case, it appears to be nature that acts, not human beings. On this model, we are back in the world of the nature religions, in which there is no real responsibility, and there can then be no real history. Human will is re-conceived as something outside of nature that then has to interfere with nature (presumably with brain function) in order for a human being to act, to make something happen.

But volokinesis as a model of action hides most of what is important in an act. When a human motion counts as a human act, and what act it counts as, are a matter of context. What counts as relevant is a matter of skill, a skill of editing, a skill of narrative, a skill of knowing, a skill of spelling out what is going on. That skill comes not from applying any laws of nature but from knowing human involvements in the world. It is true that we do, in a sense, attribute action to physical motions, but when we do that, we have always *already* picked out at least tentatively some motions as relevant and a narrative plot for the action they are part of. Human infants learn to do that as they acquire language; when humans do not acquire language, they don't develop the capacity for real action. The act is constituted *as* an act by the acts of editing that can pick it out from the background physical motions. It is not just physical motions. What an act is depends on its context, in ways we all understand intuitively, but often cannot explain. We have subtle and sophisticated skills of narrating and judging acts. We can tell what's relevant in the larger context, even when we don't know *how* we can tell. We rarely have any *theory* of how we judge acts, at least not beyond mere rules of thumb.

We can at this point look ahead a little, and finish the story about science and religion that began in the seventeenth century. There never would have been a problem of "science and religion," science would never have been in conflict with religion, if religion had not attempted to speak the language of science. When theology tries to pass off theological claims as science, trouble is bound to come. Volokinesis doesn't work, and it was only a matter of time before people saw that. There are many today who want to resuscitate volokinesis. Others try to patch up relations between science and religion, but the remedies are much the same: They want substitutes for volokinesis by putting acts of God in quantum indeterminacy (instead of outright violations of laws of nature), but the faulty presupposition remains unchallenged: that volokinesis is how God acts. If that's not how acts of God work, then the problem goes away—or never arises in the first place. But finding another way to think about acts of God has been a long and hard road, with many complex tasks along the way. It is not over yet.

Chapter 7

Postmodernity

7.1 Disestablishment and Challenge

When the social order crumbles, people have to think and act for themselves, to make choices. When they can experience their choices *as* choices, they begin to see that things really are not as self-evident as they once appeared to be. That happened in religion and philosophy at the end of the eighteenth century.

It was also a time of greatly escalated challenge to biblical religion. When doing things differently was unthinkable, there was no room for creativity—and no room for meaninglessness or chaos. Both progress and anxiety are impossible when the world cannot change. When disestablishment made change possible, both creativity and chaos followed quickly. The masters of suspicion, apostles of chaos, were Darwin, Marx, Freud, and Nietzsche. Creativity we come to later, with Schleiermacher, Kierkegaard, and the biblical scholars.

Darwin disposed of the doctrine of creation as it was understood in his time. Marx showed that much of the Christian universe was a social construction for economic reasons, and moreover was designed to support the powerful against the weak. Freud showed (or people thought he did) that psychologically, we are just animals in heat. And

Nietzsche heckled all pretenses of virtue as a cloak for the will to power. Along the way, Søren Kierkegaard was the beginning of the road back from these doubters. He faced doubt honestly and still believed—but at a philosophical cost that many even today are not willing to pay.

In the literal interpretation of the creation stories, the world was created in about 4000 BCE, by divine fiat. In nineteenth-century geology, the earth was millions of years old. Darwin's theory provided a way for humans to evolve by natural processes from other animals. His theory was only a preliminary sketch of evolution. There were vast gaps in his explanations, compared to what biologists know today, and biologists today still have many unanswered questions. But the damage to the literal account of Genesis 1–2 was done: Darwin showed how a naturalistic explanation was possible.

Darwin appeared to make man (a) just another animal, (b) not created, and so (c) just part of nature, an unattractive and desolate nature at that. Worse, especially when seen through the eyes of Thomas Huxley and Herbert Spencer, with whom Darwin largely agreed, human *social* life was a matter of "survival of the fittest," and so ruthless competition and exploitation were morally legitimate simply because they were the only way people could exist at all. This is called "Social Darwinism," and it was an excuse for the strong to abuse the weak in society. No wonder many Christians rejected the whole package. Recovering from each of these insults was and is quite possible, but it took a long time and much rethinking.

The world had already been quietly transformed in the seventeenth century in the move from medieval Christian humanism to the natural world of the modern natural sciences. In the new world, supernatural dualism was both the most and least plausible form of transcendence: It was the only form of transcendence that made sense in a naturalistic world, but it was incapable of being *true* in that world. Darwin showed that.

For theologians and historians, it was biblical scholars who wrecked the received interpretation of the Bible (we come to them in section 7.4). In the popular imagination, Darwin did the damage. He destroyed the literal truth of Genesis 1–3, and with it biblical inerrancy more generally. How could the Bible be trusted if any parts of it were false?

If Darwin pushed creation, the supernatural, and the human soul over the edge, Marx's followers began an active movement to live without transcendence of any kind. He also brought serious charges against the social order, a social order largely supported by the Church. He made the cosmos look like a fiction put out by the rich to control the poor. It was highly uncomplimentary to the received traditions.

Marx showed a social dimension of ethics that was rarely suspected before his time, and his critique of capitalist society seemed to undermine its moral legitimacy utterly. That critique was rejected in the nineteenth century as an assault on all that is good and holy. Yet in the twentieth century, Marxist ethics and economics swept the world, and still remain popular among academics in America at the start of the twenty-first century.

Marx repackaged a Deuteronomic ethic of fairness—love, in a way—but without the hope in a transcendent reality that accompanied Deuteronomic ethics in the Bible. (Deuteronomists were not the only voices in biblical ethics, but that's far from our story right now.)

Marxism has often called itself "dialectical materialism," meaning Hegelian (the dialectical part) but without Hegelian idealism (the materialist part). When Hegel went out of fashion, latter-day Marxists called themselves "historical materialists," meaning that life is historical, but the materialism still means there is no transcendence. And Marxist "love" became coercive. Coercive love without hope quickly descends into atrocities—wholesale lies, wholesale murder, and wholesale economic irrationality. The death toll at the hands of orthodox Marxist socialists in China and the Soviet Union far surpassed that of the heretical National Socialists in Germany.

Sigmund Freud pretty much demolished what passed for psychology before his time, and psychology since has been as suspicious of Freud as Freud was of psychology before his time. To deal adequately with Freud would take another book, one I could not write. Suffice it to say that he reminded people (positively) that we are bodies as well as spirits, and that the body is not evil. In practice (whatever Freudian theory may have been), psychoanalysis often worked as a way of fixing broken narratives, life-stories, even if it lacked the resources of a Christian universe into which to put those life stories. On the other hand, after Freud, we appeared to be animals made of lust, lust all the way down. It's not clear whether Freud was the cause or merely the excuse for changes in sexual ethics in the twentieth century. A theology of the body we do not have; recovering such a Christian perspective on embodiment was one of the projects of John Paul II. Like Freud, it is too much for this book.

It is worth note that Freud's psychology treated human existence as just nature, without spirit or history. It contained the seeds of a return to nature religion as a basic life orientation. Freud was followed by Carl Jung, a candid reviver of the mimetic archetypes (section 2.3) that animated ancient nature religions.

In each attack on the religious tradition, the supposedly anti-Christian thinker selectively borrowed biblical themes and used them against biblical religion. With both Darwin and the Bible, we come from nature, and nature is not divine, nor is nature entirely benevolent. With both Marx and the Bible, we are both social and historical beings, and we do have ethical obligations to all members of society, the poor especially. With both Freud and the Bible, narrative matters in human lives, we are embodied, with bodily appetites and drives, and the body is good and not evil.

The problems with each of these critics were more what they left out than what they asserted. They showed that transcendence by means of a supernatural doesn't work. The modern supernatural was a recent invention (no older than the 1600s), though the nineteenth century thought it went all the way back to Moses. To rule out any other kind of transcendence, as readers of Darwin, Marx, and Freud did, was to jump to conclusions recklessly. We are still recovering from the modern supernatural, still recovering a transcendence that is not just naturalism by other means.

Darwin, Marx, Freud, and Nietzsche were a threat to supernaturalism and to the social order. The biblical scholars that we come to shortly were obscure, technical, hard to understand, and easy to ignore. The world that was publicly threatened was the world of the supernatural, the world of volokinetic divine action, the naturalization of transcendence, and colloquial Platonist dualism. Friedrich Nietzsche, the Lord of Nihilism, belongs with the twentieth century, for much of which he can stand as the icon.

7.2 Nihilism and the Century of Destruction

Friedrich Nietzsche was a preacher's kid, and as PKs often are, a trouble-maker. He knew the classics as well as Lutheran theology. He wrote, and people didn't like what he wrote. He seemed to make fun of the virtues of Victorian Liberal Germany. They had promoted a culture of idealism and altruism. He said that idealism and altruism were a cover for will to power. Thus far, he might have passed for a conventional Lutheran pastor preaching about sin. People were quite used to hearing and ignoring charges of hypocrisy—and then piously thanking the preacher for his sermons.

So Nietzsche said, or at least his readers heard, "Why *not* will to power, why not deception, why not stiff the poor?" To make that truly infuriating, you have to make it sound like you mean it. He may have meant it; I can't tell.

Let me update Nietzsche's message, at least as it was heard, for our own time. Nietzsche was a German, brought up on Plato and philosophy. So when he went on a tirade, he attacked philosophy. If he had been English, he would have attacked the Church at another point, its liturgy. R. F. Laird, in *The Boomer Bible*, did exactly that. "Harry" is the First-Born Babe of the Boom, the first of the boomer generation:

> High and Mighty Harry, We will be following your Way on this day, in blind obedience to the devices and desires of our own hearts. We may, from time to time, break sundry laws. We may leave undone those things which others will say we ought to have done; And we may do those things which others will say we ought not to have done. But that is the way we are, O Chief, and we know that none of these omissions and commissions can possibly be our fault, or our responsibility to correct or atone for, . . .

It is a satire on all the works and pomps of my generation, the Baby Boomers. Those who grew up on the 1928 Book of Common Prayer will recognize it instantly—and so can both enjoy it and be grossed out by it; for of course the correct words are,

> Almighty and most merciful Father; we have erred, and strayed from thy ways like lost sheep. We have followed too much the devices and desires of our own hearts. . . . We have left undone those things which we ought to have done; And we have done those things which we ought not to have done; And there is no health in us. . . .

Laird's satire would be hard to mistake for promotion of what it literally says. That is, it would be hard to *get away* with taking it that way. But you could. And the possibility of taking it literally is so exquisitely tempting that you couldn't miss it.

That's what some of Nietzsche's readers did with his very similar message. He said that a will not to deceive is underneath it all a will to die. The will to power is good. And pity makes suffering contagious. (Pretty much takes care of all three of exposure, limitation, and need, doesn't it?) And so along came the Nazis, and they took Nietzsche as license to defy truth and ride over all opposition. Nietzsche despised anti-semites, but the anti-semites loved Nietzsche.

Eugen Rosenstock-Huessy once said that when the parents are decadent, the children are condemned to barbarism. 1890–1910, the height of Victorian Liberal society, was followed by 1914–1945. More broadly, we can sorrow at how the nineteenth century was followed by the twentieth.

Nietzsche's diagnosis was right: European society was in trouble. It was decadent, but more than just decadent. Accusing it of will to power doesn't go deep enough. It would be more accurate to say that, for Western society, will to power is all there is; will to power is where it's at, the only thing that matters. (The charge still fits, so don't think things are all of a sudden a whole lot better.) And Rosenstock-Huessy was right, too, if in hindsight: barbarism follows decadence as night follows day. With decadence, the veils that cover will to power wore thin and you could see what life was all about, beneath the pretenses. With the pretenses gone, what was left could be candid. Will to power? Of course! Eliminate the weak? Of course! Starting with the Jews.

Well, yes and no. The pogroms against the Jews in Germany followed a long tradition in European history. They were organized by people who took Nietzsche as their blessing. When the first wholesale killing started, it was not the Jews but the disabled who got killed (Burleigh and Gallagher). Gas chambers, using carbon monoxide, were built at a few hospitals, and about half of the institutionalized disabled in Germany were killed between 1939 and 1941. (The program was officially halted in 1941, but it did not stop; when the war was over, 85% of the institutionalized disabled were gone, and they were not killed by the National Socialists, but by their doctors.) The gas chambers for the disabled were scaled up in 1941, with hydrogen cyanide, for use on the Jews, at Auschwitz. The disabled were merely *Leben unlebenswert*; the Jews were considered beneath that. The Germans have learned from their experience. Today, the problems are in the Low Countries, Switzerland, and Oregon.

The Holocaust, as it is commonly called, or just The Destruction, the Shoah in Hebrew, attracts singular attention in the modern mind. One could miss the *other* places where large numbers of people were eliminated. Often *more* people than the Jews that the National Socialists eliminated from Eastern Europe. Stalin eliminated many millions of people in the Soviet Union who were economically unnecessary and socially or politically inconvenient; and similarly under Mao in China. (R. J. Rummel's *Death by Government* tells some of the story.)

Yet the Holocaust rightly preoccupies us, because even though it was not the largest genocide in terms of bodycount, it was a betrayal at a level deeper than the others. Christians are supposed to share a common tradition with Jews, and for Christians to eliminate Jews is a betrayal of loyalty owed both to Jews and to Christian principles. The perpetrators were no longer really Christian, yet they came from a Christian culture, and the Nazis had help in the form of collusion and silence from many Christians.

What comes as a surprise is that the English-speaking world is in many ways the mother of eliminating surplus people. In the English-speaking world, it has usually been disorganized, scattered, private instead of institutionalized, or just absent-minded, which makes it all the more surprising when it is pointed out. (It continues in abortion and the movement to legalize euthanasia today.) Richard Rubenstein tells the story, and sizes up modern European civilization as one that *habitually* eliminates people, if usually without spelling out what it is doing. When previously common and open agricultural lands were enclosed in the fifteenth and sixteenth centuries, many people were put out of work. They were moved to cities, to poverty, put in poorhouses, sent to the colonies, or hanged. In the nineteenth century, half the Irish were starved or driven into exile. (The English "needed" more space.) Little if any of this was explicitly intended or planned by the government. Later, in America, clearing the land meant getting rid of both trees and natives; there was not much difference between them. Hitler was merely copying the English in Ireland; he needed more space. In order to grind Catholic Poland into the dust, it was expedient to eliminate the people whom Catholic Poles looked down upon, Jewish Poles. That way, Catholic Poles might be more efficiently bullied into accepting their lot.

Christians ask, these days, what was it about Christian Europe that made possible such embarrassing atrocities? That takes a little digging. Christians were not supposed to be killing Jews, at least not on the basis of accepted and official policy. For at the end time, all the Jews were supposed to convert to Christianity, and the Synagogue would go out of business. (Today, sixty years after the Shoah, that is embarrassing theology, but it was accepted everywhere until recently, and still is, in some places.)

We have seen the basic story, the history of how the Church and the Synagogue each rebuilt after the destruction of the Second Temple, how they became gradually separated and estranged from each other, how each developed ways to disinherit the other. I think the answer to my question, what is it about Christianity that made this killing possible, is something inherent in historical religion. It is built into the anxiety of history: the possibility of rejecting that anxiety, and rebelling against it. If you can tell yourself and your neighbors that you are the One True Church, the One And Only People of God, then you can escape from a lot of anxiety. That's what people are poking fun at when they laugh at you. Their laughter exposes your anxiety.

Where does that anxiety come from? If you make up your religion, anxiety is natural. And we saw that biblical religion of the Christian variety is indeed made-up: We saw that in *Unwelcome Good News*, in section 6.1, "Children's Games." And the origins in Israelite religion are equally made-up: We saw that in *By the Waters of Naturalism*, section 6.5, "$\pi = 4$." That made-up-ness is the model for covenantal religion ever since.

We saw early that the move from nature to history was a move from security to dread. One of the reasons for that dread is just exactly the freedom that comes with history. There's more than one way to cut a covenant. Call it a responsible liberty of interpretation: you have to negotiate some, with your neighbors, they will yell if you step on their toes, but to a large extent, you get to make up the rules as you go along. You can't kick people out of the community of moral obligation, you have to live more or less within the seven lessons of the Exodus, you have to affirm human life in history in this world. But that doesn't by any means tell you how to do everything, as all the disagreements among sectarian Judaisms and sectarian Christianities well attest.

So in the end, what does the Destruction of European Judaism tell us? At least this much: It reminds us (because we had denied it) how much Christianity has in common with rabbinic Judaism, i. e., that Christianity is an Exodus tradition. It tells us that Christianity should honor the Other Exodus tradition. And it tells us that our religion is our own artifact. We have to live with that. We do have a responsible liberty of interpretation in the conduct of a covenant, and after two thousand years of denial, it might not be too soon to face that fact. It is not a bug but a feature of covenantal religion that there are different varieties of it, varieties that can't agree. (*Elementary Monotheism*, section 7.4 is a somewhat dry explanation: schism, apart from its bitterness and rancor, is not always a bad thing.)

7.3 The Road Back

The road back from the despairs of nihilism and the supernatural has been (and doubtless will be still) a long one. The road to recovery begins with nineteenth-century theologians and biblical scholars. The biblical scholars we come to momentarily. First, and all too briefly, two theologians who stand at the headwaters of their century: Schleiermacher and Kierkegaard.

Friedrich Schleiermacher (1768–1834), the father of German Liberal Theology, was a contemporary of Hegel (1770–1831). Much easier to read than Kierkegaard, he nonetheless leaves more difficult problems unsolved. His instinct was to start theology with what you can see, in this world and not some other. In that he was right. The trouble, so far as I can understand it, is that Liberal Theology never really was able to make much sense of transcendence. I shall not be fair to Liberal Theology, mostly because we omit its story here, a long and rich story. Claude Welch tells it well. My complaints against Liberal Theology can wait until we come to it as a living option today (in section 8.2). Schleiermacher's initial instinct was, so far as I can see, all to the good: do theology without recourse to a supernatural; look for some other form of transcendence. I don't think he or his heirs looked very seriously; they certainly didn't find one.

Søren Kierkegaard is another matter. Consummately frustrating, full of irony yet tantalizing, he did put his finger on the root issue in transcendence: hope. The contrast to hope is despair, and the temptation of his age (and ours, still) is despair in face of the appearance of no transcendence, no God, no home for man in the universe. Kierkegaard was reacting to Hegel, who made history seem too systematic, too predictable, too easy. Kierkegaard nonetheless in his way followed the course recommended by Schleiermacher: he thought his way through theology without a supernatural, just looking at what people do when they hope and when they despair. (Much easier to read than Kierkegaard is Josef Pieper, *On Hope*, by the way.) Two books stand out. *Sickness Unto Death* is about hope and despair, and the *Concluding Unscientific Postscript* does, in its strange way, I suppose, help us a little with transcendence.

In *Sickness Unto Death*, Kierkegaard asks what a human self is, and answers that it is a "relationship that relates itself to itself," but one that is constituted by an Other. (I care about myself, but I was constituted as one who can care about myself by circumstances beyond my control.) Despair consists in refusing to even try to be the self that one has been given to be, or in insisting on being some other self (a self of one's own making) instead of the self that one has been given to be. They are the despair of apathy and the despair of defiance, if you will. Kierkegaard is unsurpassed in his portrayal of them, and of how the soul is trapped in despair until it consents to be a self constituted by an Other, rather than keep trying to be the self of the devices and desires of its own heart, ever so pious though those devices and desires might be. (Many questions Kierkegaard did not ask: "How can I *tell* what self I have been given to be?" is only one.)

In Thomistic or Aristotelian terms, the two despairs are the lack of a virtue (hope) or its excess. Hope, then, if I can conjecture a reading of both Kierkegaard and Aquinas, is the active and committed desire that God will be God (Thomas Aquinas, *Summa Theologiae* ii-ii.17.2), or in other words, that God will be good and good to us, without setting limits or conditions on *how* God is to do that. Yet Aquinas is not particularly helpful because he thinks in terms of a Platonist cosmos that cannot today escape from the supernaturalism of the modern world. Kierkegaard and postmodernity have to be faced on their own terms.

There is more than a little trust in the virtue of hope, else the believing soul cannot become a self that rests content in its constitution by another. That trust is a subjective thing (such is the message of the *Postscript*), and in that subjectivity is the soul's relationship to God. It is not, contrary to the modern supernatural, an objective thing, yet that subjective relationship still relates to something real outside the subject. This is neither subjectivism nor objectivism.

A little more can be said about hope. It is not speculation about the "after-life" (that is something best left to God). Hope is the ability to bear major disappointments, injustice even, confident that all the pains and wrongs of life can be and in some sense are fitted into a coherent whole that is good, even if its goodness is not yet visible. This is quite dangerous, for you can use it (misuse it, actually) to get the disadvantaged to bear their disadvantages willingly, just as Marx said. There is a counter-thesis that was popular in the 1960s, that "all you need is love." On the contrary, Stanley Hauerwas replied, all the difficult moral issues are questions about "whom to hurt with justice." But people disagree about what a just distribution of assets and disadvantages is. Inability to bear disappointment, however, can be used to justify whatever level of violence is necessary to correct perceived injustice. Atrocities in the name of justice, in a word. The attempt to practice the virtue of love without hope (i. e., Marxism) has resulted in atrocities beyond belief.

We are now in a position to diagnose the two despairs of nihilism and the supernatural. Nihilism is the refusal to even try to be the self one has been given to be: here, to be the Christian society the modern world has enabled. For nihilism, nothing means anything, and anything goes. The supernatural, conceived in pious faith, is trickier. Instead of accepting transcendence that is not under control, it sought an objective transcendence, against the tradition of wiser heads in theology. We shall see more of that as our story unfolds further.

Our theme so far is that when the old world tottered after the medieval synthesis, some tried to build a new and different one (the seventeenth century supernatural), some tried to save it (the supernatural yet again, in the nineteenth century), but both failed. The old hope was gone, and a new one was not yet born. The resources were not there yet. In the meantime, despair came—first as a threat and a spectre in the nineteenth century, then as savage destruction in the twentieth. Nevertheless, the old hope was corrupt and had to go. It was a transcendence domesticated and then compromised by naturalism, nature religions, and attempts to escape the limitations of creaturehood in this life.

We have passed over many nineteenth century thinkers, and most of the details. Like the Deuteronomic Historian in an earlier age, we concentrate on a few figures and their contributions for or against theology. Unlike the Deuteronomic Historian, our tale is not one of cycles of unredeemed degeneration ending in disaster. (We are not there yet.) For some the nineteenth century has been permission to dilute or abandon world-affirming historical religion, returning to religions of nature, the perennial philosophy, or exilic religions (cf.

section 5.6 above). But for others, the nineteenth century opened the way to a recovery of biblical religion at a level much deeper than anything previously suspected. How it will all play out is unknown, because that's still in the future. Our task right now is to get to know our own present a little better.

7.4 First We Destroy Your Faith

In section 2.1, we began the results of modern scholarship, but deferred the story of how those results were achieved. It is time to tell that story, as beginning students in seminary hear it. In the beginning Bible course, the first thing they learn is about the composition and editing of the Bible: Who put it together, and when, all that we covered in chapters 3 and 4. The modern part of the story is about who figured out who put the Bible together, and when. Many then think the Bible was not written by God, because we know roughly who *did* write it. The experience can be a big downer, and it can be exhilarating. Some feel like their faith has been abused, and they lampoon their teachers in the wisecrack, "First, we destroy your faith." But if you do your homework, that's not how it ends.

Fortress Press put out a series of short pamphlets, guides to biblical scholarship, in the 1970s. The contribution by Edgar Krentz, *The Historical-Critical Method*, is a good place for anyone to start. The story begins in the eighteenth century, with a few hints before. Scholars looked at biblical manuscripts more carefully and with particular attention to inconsistencies, seeking clues to how the texts were assembled. Before the 1600s, the Bible was *the* authority on every topic it touched. In that century, the Bible began to lose its authority, because people learned independently that many things were not as the Bible said they were. That the earth goes around the sun instead of the other way around is only the most famous.

The inquirers were on the whole a faithful lot, and they tried to salvage as much of the Bible as possible on literal terms. A small patch in the story here, a detail there, and you could still read the Bible as before. Prayer would not be unduly disturbed. The critics did not have an easy time of it, the public was not impressed, but where the critics first asked questions, others soon followed.

What came after was, in its way, a war between "faith" and "reason," and the field of battle was the text of the Bible. In 1670, Benedict Baruch Spinoza, a Jew living in Amsterdam, published the *Tractatus Theologico-Politicus*. He was trying to make peace. He argued that the Bible ignores the ordinary natural causes the new sciences were discovering, in order to speak of God and the relation between God and humans. Apparent violations of laws of nature in the Bible meant nothing; they did not happen, and the texts are trying to tell you something quite other than the report of an event. The trouble with this is that it makes the Bible into a liar—if you think it is intended to be literally true. The pious reading public wouldn't have it. But Spinoza opened the way to the new critical history, and he was in many ways the father of the biblical scholarship that came after him.

Before long, someone noticed that Moses dies before the end of the books that he supposedly wrote. Then people noticed that the Gospels contradict each other in places, and they suspected that Isaiah was a composite collection of writings not all from one hand. Then someone thought that Moses was an editor, not just God's secretary. As an editor, he worked with older sources, or "reminiscences."

This sort of stuff attracts wild imaginations, and before long, someone (his name was Reimarus) thought that Jesus was a deluded visionary, preaching the end of the world. That was published under a pen name, because the author was (rightly) cautious about publishing in his own name. Reimarus opened up the nineteenth-century investigation into the Gospels. Life-of-Jesus research was created in outraged response to him.

In the nineteenth century, secular history and biblical history proceed apace in tandem. And for secular history, the history of the Greeks and Romans, no texts were sacred, and so method could be tried out with impunity. It was not always secular history that pioneered the innovations, but when it did, it was less controversial. People worked on the Bible because it was the history they really cared about. The Old Testament, as the Common Documents were read in the Church, was just second-class enough in its sacredness and at the same time interesting enough so that Christians both cared about it and still could question it. In a major way, this was a Lutheran contribution, for Lutherans have a mysticism of the power of the Word unsurpassed in any other Christian community. The purpose was no longer to be edifying, but to answer critical questions: what is the correct reading of the text, how was it put together, and when?

In 1835, David Friedrich Strauss published his *Life of Jesus*, and it was translated into English by George Eliot in 1846. He entertained the possibility that the New Testament was speaking in mythological language. The end of literal readings was at hand, for now you could ask about other ways to read the text, other ways it could have been intended. (The text might even pull your leg.) A little more, and people could see that the Gospels were written by editors who had their own theologies, and whose editorial choices reflected those theologies.

Remember, in *Waters*, in "Happy Easter," the list of the miracles in Mark? How they start out with first just a hand, and work up by stages to whole-body healings and then raisings from the dead? That tells you something: these are edited documents. It also put the fear into people, that these texts might be like the radio evangelist's line that we began with: simply fabricated stories. People were understandably alarmed and offended. David Friedrich Strauss lost his job (he was not the first, nor the last).

In 1878, Julius Wellhausen published a *History of Israel*, and in it laid out the four-source hypothesis that has, with variations, come down to us today as "JEDP." Later, more tentative, it became in 1885 the *Prolegomena to the History of Israel*. Karl Heinrich Graf had earlier argued that Leviticus and portions of Genesis and Exodus pertinent to it were written *after* the Babylonian Exile, i.e., later than 540 BCE.

Moses lived in 1200 BCE or earlier. Leviticus deals with matters that were a concern after the Exile, but hardly for Moses. Wellhausen took over the idea from Graf and others, made it a little more orderly.

The "documentary hypothesis," as it is called, says that there were four sources in the Pentateuch, and they are called by letters, J, E, D, and P. We have seen those four sources in Chapters 3 and 4. J and E use the words Jahweh and Elohim for the name of God. D is for Deuteronomy, and P is the Priestly editor. The documentary hypothesis has been a fairly hardy theory. That said, confidence in it is not what it once was. But the characteristic differences between D, P, and the "other" material are stubbornly visible. J and E are frequently hard to tell apart, and there is much material that is earlier than D and P, but not otherwise assignable with certainty. What does survive of the documentary hypothesis is confidence that the biblical texts are edited, and from multiple sources: they are the work of a community, not a single author, and they grew over a period of many centuries.

In the beginning, professors tell the new students how the story was put together. Since Wellhausen's name is the label for the JEDP theory, one could say, "in the beginning was Julius Wellhausen." But it is not just the names, Wellhausen, Graf, Gunkel, Noth, von Rad, and so on, mostly Germans and all unknown outside seminaries. It is texts in the Bible, starting with the clues about the names of God, but much, much more than just that. It is now out of date, but a little guide by H. H. Rowley, *The Growth of the Old Testament* (1950), nicely summarizes the evidence.

In the first place, there are anachronisms, things that don't make sense on the theory that Moses wrote the "Five Books of Moses." It is not just that Moses himself died in the end of Deuteronomy; that could have been added by a later editor without greatly compromising the tradition that the whole collection was a unitary collection, from one author, one inspired scribe. Genesis 36:31 lists Edomite kings who ruled before any Israelite king; but Moses himself could not have known there would be Israelite kings. Genesis 12:6 and 13:7 speak of a time when the Canaanite was in the land, and can only have been written afterward, during the Israelite occupation, after the time of Moses. These are small things, but they are odd, and they are in the middle of the texts, not on the edges of them, at the beginnings or endings of stories.

In the second place, many incidents appear in two or three versions. When I was first reading these documents in the schedule of the Lectionary of the 1928 Prayerbook in 1973 and 1974, even I noticed that something was up when the same stories reappeared in different versions. A patriarch passes his wife off as his sister in order to survive among hostile neighbors not once but three times (Genesis 12:10, 20:1, 26:6). Luz is renamed Bethel more than once (Genesis 28:19, 35:14). Jacob is renamed Israel twice, in two different places, once at Bethel, and once on the east side of the Jordan river, at the ford of the Jabbok (Genesis 35:10, 32:29).

In the third place, there are contradictions. The creation stories in Genesis 1 and 2 are inconsistent: were man and woman created together at the end, or were animals and plants created after man and before woman? In Genesis 37, was Joseph sold to Ishmaelites or to Midianites? These are only some of the contradictions.

In the fourth place, there are disagreements in law. Compare Exodus 20:24 and Deuteronomy 12:14: many altars, or only one?

In the fifth place is the divine name. There are not merely different names, but the statements *about* the divine name raise problems. In Exodus 6:2–3, God says to Moses,

> I am Jahweh. To Abraham and Isaac and Jacob I appeared as El Shaddai; I did not make myself known to them by my name Jahweh (Jerusalem Bible, alt.).

You're the first person to whom I've ever told my real name; no-one else has ever heard it before. But of course the name is common in Genesis. And in Genesis 15:7, he says to Abraham, "I am Jahweh"; in 28:13, to Jacob, the same words. What gives?

In the sixth place there is a noticeably different conception of God in the first and second accounts of creation. In the second, God looks like a human; in the first, he is very abstract and lofty.

In the seventh place, there are other characteristic differences of style. Deuteronomy, for example, is almost unique unto itself. And one could go on; these are a mere sample of the texts Rowley cites, and the technical literature has many more. Sorting things out, one gets the four sources in the JEDP hypothesis.

You might then go on to ask, how did these traditions get put together, how did J and E work, where did they get their material? That means looking at how oral traditions work. Nothing is so convincing as an experience in real life. In my senior year in high-school, I and a friend, Scott Anderson, built a half-finished seismograph. We were defeated by the modest mathematics necessary to calculate how to capture and amplify a signal that could be fed to a chart recorder. Years later, at a class reunion, I heard what we had "done" from another friend. It seems we had built not a failed seismograph but a working cyclotron, an atom-smasher. Thus do oral traditions grow. And when I was a boy, on Mackinac Island in Michigan, and I used to listen to the tour guides chanting their spiel for the tourists as they drove past various historic spots on the Island. The priests telling the pilgrims about Jacob at the Jabbok and again also at Bethel must have sounded very much the same. It's like all the colonial American inns that advertise, "George Washington slept here."

When I was first teaching these things to students in the School for Deacons in San Francisco, California, I divided the class up into three groups, told them to go out and find news clippings, original texts wherever they could get them, and edit together the history of the school; or in another year, the beginnings of American history. Each group had an editor, who retyped everything so that the rest of us could not tell from mere appearance how the editing had been done. Copies of the three accounts were distributed to the whole class. And as a class, we tried to reconstruct the editing of the different accounts, without knowing how each group had done their work. The results were very much like JEDP: Some contributions were easy to spot, some were very hard to disentangle. Having lived (or recreated) the documentary hypothesis in their own experience, it was not just obvious, they were comfortable with it. The documentary hypothesis may or may not withstand scholars' attacks, but it is pretty clear that the texts we have in the Pentateuch are edited documents, from diverse earlier sources. My students experienced both the thrills and the uncertainties of modern scholarship. Even undergraduates can do this, and they liked it, too. To be fair, when I taught this stuff, we always also went through the arguments about how each biblical editor presented good news in his own time and place, as we saw above in Chapters 3 and 4. When some theology accompanies the textual archaeology, it is possible to accept the documentary hypothesis as good news and an offer of grace, not as a condemnation and exposure of biblical religion as a fraud. Julius Wellhausen was not the grinch who stole the Bible (or God). His successors who reconstructed the history of Israelite religion have made that amply clear. They did not make it unreal, they made it real in terms of the modern world.

The fact that the documentary hypothesis has attracted a lot of skepticism recently does not change much: The last third of the twentieth century has seen a great caution about reconstructing textual history. Dating is not as obvious as it once was. P and D remain fairly distinct, but separating J, E, and "other" non-P, non-D material doesn't command the confidence it once did. Nevertheless, it is still pretty clear that the tradition of Exodus and settlement of the Land, leading to the Monarchy, was the matrix into which the other traditions were fitted: the Patriarchal history in Genesis, and the Sinai and Law traditions in the rest of the Pentateuch.

What emerges from the archaeology of the biblical texts is a new history of Israel. The period before the book of Joshua is extremely murky, though not thereby without any historical basis at all. Only with the monarchy, the time of David and Solomon, is the historian on even semi-firm ground. Before and during the monarchy we see the transformation of aboriginal nature religion into a historical religion. It flowered in the life of the first Temple, Solomon's Temple. After disaster, returning from the Exile, the Jews rebuilt the Temple, and this time they kept their religion pretty much clean of idol worship. Things muddled along, sometimes happy, sometimes not, until the next disaster, the destruction of the Second Temple by the Romans in 70 CE.

Behind it all was the story of the Exodus, in ways that are not intuitive at all. The reconstruction of the role of the Exodus in the texts goes well beyond the mere reconstruction of how the Common Documents were edited, when, and by whom. It was work done in the twentieth century. The next part of the story is the integration of the Common Documents and the New Testament, the Exodus and the Gospels, and their place in the larger history of religions.

7.5 Exodus Again, Again

The story of the Exodus as a crossing from nature religion into historical religion we saw above, in chapters 3 and 4. In section 4.4 we found seven lessons in the Exodus, lessons that have shaped radical monotheism ever since. We are in the middle of the story of how this history was rediscovered in the last two centuries.

Twentieth-century scholars saw how central the Exodus is, in both the Common Documents and the New Testament (its role underlying the Mishnah and the Talmuds goes without saying). Christians had traditionally read the "Old" Testament with the prophets at the center, because the prophets prophesy Jesus, and Jesus is what's most important. But that's not how the Common Documents were written or organized. The Exodus is at the center.

It took major work to see that, to place the texts in a larger coherent whole. Traditionally, among Jews, the books of Joshua, Judges, Samuel and Kings are known as the Former Prophets. The later prophets are Isaiah, Jeremiah, Ezekiel, and the twelve minor prophets (Hosea to Micah). (Daniel is not one of the prophets at all, but a late work of fiction, even though Christian Bibles print the book among the prophets.) The Former Prophets tell the story of the road to the Israelite monarchy and its eventual destruction by the Assyrians and the Babylonians.

Two scholars stand out in recovering the structure of the Pentateuch and Former Prophets. Gerhard von Rad published an essay with a daunting title, "The Form-Critical Problem of the Hexateuch," in 1938, on the Exodus as the structure or backbone that ties together everything that happens from Genesis to Second Kings.

Running through that story is the nutshell summary that von Rad found in the "short historical creed," Deuteronomy 26:5b–9:

> A wandering Aramean was my father; and he went down into Egypt and sojourned there, few in number; and there he became a nation, great, mighty, and populous. And the Egyptians treated us harshly, and afflicted us, and laid upon us hard bondage. Then we cried out to the LORD the God of our fathers, and the LORD heard our voice, and saw our affliction, our toil, and our oppression; and the LORD brought us out of Egypt with a mighty hand and an outstretched arm, with great terror, with signs and wonders; and he brought us into this place and gave us this land, a land flowing with milk and honey. (von Rad, pp. 3–4, altered in the divine name).

This sketch of the story, the leaving of Egypt and entry into the promised Land, omitting Sinai and the Law, is the usual form of other summaries until very late texts that insert the Law into the wilderness adventures, as Nehemiah does, but Psalms 78, 105 and 106 do not. The texts in Exodus are an edited synthesis of the two traditions, one of the wilderness, one of the Law. Both kinds come from multiple sources: J, E, and P, with not much D until the book of Deuteronomy.

The second major change in reading the Common Documents came in 1943, when Martin Noth published "The Deuteronomistic History," showing the links in theology, editing, and style between the books of Deuteronomy and the Former Prophets. The books of Joshua to Second Kings (except for Ruth) were originally one history, with a common theme and a common purpose, that came from people close to Deuteronomy and Jeremiah. The commands in Deuteronomy set up the program that was sometimes followed, more often flouted in the history of the monarchy, from Samuel to Kings, ending in the destruction of the monarchy as divine punishment for disobedience. The history has no interest in the details of worship that one finds in the P texts of Leviticus and Numbers, but a great interest in faithfulness to the one God and avoidance of all other gods. The promises and obligations in Deuteronomy are followed through the Former Prophets. Sometimes Israel kept its obligations, sometimes not. In the end, not, and the promises were revoked: that is the explanation of the fall of the kingdoms of Israel and Judah.

If the reading of the Pentateuch and Former Prophets was transformed in those years, the view of other religions was transformed also. As we saw in section 2.3, Mircea Eliade tumbled to the differences between religions of nature and religions of history. In the 1930s and 1940s, he had been studying aboriginal religions in Asia, and he found consistent themes in such religions, themes different from biblical religion. He published *Cosmos and History* in 1949. In a nature religion, it is really nature that drives human actions and human lives. In a historical religion, people are responsible for their actions as they cannot be in nature alone, despite the uncertainty in their lives. Anxiety in history is one result.

In the 1970s Merold Westphal taught a course in beginning philosophy of religion, and relied on (among others) Eliade's comparisons. The result was *God, Guilt, and Death* (1984). Its last chapters contain the core of the menu of religious choices that we saw in section 5.6 above. It was Westphal who observed that in a nature religion, the cosmogony is the model for human life ever after, but in a historical religion, the beginnings in nature are just a prologue to history. That is the relation of Genesis 1–11 to the patriarchal history and the Exodus that follows it.

Once the difference between nature religions and historical religion is seen, it is easy to spot the progression from nature to history in the Pentateuch and the Former Prophets. Early on, the hallmarks of nature religion (visible idols) are still present, and the images of other gods last from the time of Jacob and Rachel to the last days of the temple in Ezekiel. What was known as shamanism in nature religions was transformed by stages into ecstatic prophecy and then ethical prophecy and theology of history. But in the early stages divination and prediction of the future for devout clients is very much in evidence. In a nature religion, the future is predictable. In a historical religion, the future is not entirely predictable, and you are still responsible for your actions. The anxieties of living in history are projected back onto the Exodus, but then the Exodus texts, though about an early time, were edited late.

This is not an evolutionary theory of religion, as if religious development were guaranteed to produce better and better religions. The choice between orienting life to nature, history, meditation, escape, or anything else always remains a *choice*. And the choices bear striking parallels through the ages.

One conclusion for those in a historical religion: a people in history is a people on pilgrimage, on a journey, but a journey whose future is unknown. The most that can be said is that the future holds the grace of God just as the past has, and that is a matter of faith, not evidence or deduction. The words for being on a pilgrimage are being *in statu viatoris*, on the way of a traveler, just passing through.

We saw in section 4.7 a set of parallels between the Exodus story and the Gospels: Jesus is the new Israel, both Israels go down to Egypt, leave Egypt, are tested and fed in the desert, cross the Jordan at Jericho, and enter the promised land. Since you already know the older story, the Exodus, you can now see the newer story, the Jesus story, as a new Exodus. Its ending in fiasco is then quite ironic—for clearly the gospel writers don't think it was a fiasco, pointless and futile, as the Greek-speaking secular public would have seen it.

Neither story is code for the other, but the message of the later story is that what God did for you in earlier times, he is doing for you again. The literary form is not quite the same thing as parody, though we have called it that in this book—*reverent* parody. It is known technically as *typology*. Many scholars have seen Exodus typology in the Gospels, going back (in modern times) at least to the nineteenth century. But it was usually just a verse here, a verse there, some unlabeled quotes and allusions in the Gospel texts, or a brief story with parallels in the Common Documents. Edward Hobbs is one of two that I know of who have seen the large-scale parallels between the synoptic Gospels and the Exodus, parallels at the level of *structure*. (Meredith Kline is the other).

Exodus typology was discovered by modern biblical scholars doing life-of-Jesus research and asking themselves what they could trust in the Gospels as solid history. When they noticed that some of the gospel narratives are shaped by Old Testament parallels, they soon noticed a lot more. Then they realized that the Gospels are edited documents just as much as the Pentateuch was. They are not just simple accounts of historical facts in temporal sequence, they are put together to advertise a way of living. They are not proofs of Jesus' divinity, they are a challenge and an invitation.

The parallels to the Exodus story are systematic, and they shape the entire Gospel story. If you want to understand Jesus the way the Gospel writers understood Jesus, you have to understand the Exodus, and you have to understand it in Greek (or have help from those who do), in the Greek translation of the Common Documents known as the Septuagint. Unlike Latin, Greek spells the names Jesus and Joshua the same way: *Iesous*. (Latin has *Iosue* and *Iesu*). And so when you hear the Gospels in Greek, you are hearing about Joshua all over again, and

Joshua was the one who led Israel into the promised land.

Edward Hobbs more than fifty years ago put together many resources to emphasize that in the Gospels, Jesus promises good in the pains of life, and does so in a characteristic pattern. Hobbs began with Karl Barth's commentary on Romans, in which Barth says that life's No is, deep down, God's Yes. The flag-text is Romans 8:28, which we saw on p. 77, but the theme occurs everywhere. It's in the Talmud, too: Are we to bless God for the evils in life as we do for the good? Yes, in a word (Bavli, Berakhot 60b).

Hobbs also tumbled to the similarity between the Gospel miracle stories and modern TV advertisements; they both are advertising a product. In the gospels, the product is in the teaching: Exposure, limitation, and need bring blessings; they are not barren, however much we would like to be excused from them.

From comparative mythology and comparative linguistics, Hobbs knew that writers in Greek (unlike Hebrew) often tend to think in three-part terms, where one part is about legitimacy and order, the second is about action, and the third is about nutrition and sustenance. These are the primary concerns of God the Son, God the Father, and God the Holy Spirit, though the Persons of the Trinity do trade work among themselves to some extent. Hobbs combined these with Barth's observation about God turning life's No into a Yes. In the first part, about legitimacy and order, God brings good out of occasions when we are shown up as not legitimate, not in order: *exposed*, caught red-handed. Exposure confronts you with the truth, and the truth can set you free. Exposure offers a chance to change, and freedom from the past. In the second part, God brings good out of the *limitations* of life, the response to which is creativity. In the third part, encounter with other people's *need*, God offers community, fellowship, and mutual support. These are not the only pains of life, but they are different enough from each other that most problems can be apportioned among exposure, limitation, and need.

In the Jesus story, then, as it was shaped late in the first century,

Jesus leads the people into a new promise, not a land but a way of living in history after the destruction of the Temple. In it, the pains of life bear blessings, often though we cannot yet see those blessings. This is a "portable" way of life, not dependent on the Land or the Temple. Rabbinic Judaism, it should be noted, handled the same problem in a similar way, also producing a portable way to continue the Exodus covenant without the Temple.

Chapter 8

Choices Today

8.1 Non-Biblical Choices

The medieval West was shaped by biblical religion in a time when there were few other choices, and none that were practical. (Muslims lived someplace else, and migration between the Church and the Synagogue was effectively suppressed.) Today, all religious options are available, and most are chosen by at least a few. Yet most were available in late antiquity also (section 5.6).

Most conspicuous among them are many ways of reviving aboriginal nature religions or devising modern analogs of them, (1) on p. 101. In a nature religion, history is unreal, irrelevant, unknowable, or just evil, the source of troubles. This world (as nature) is, up to a point, affirmable as good. Fulfillment, success in life, consists in fitting into nature naturally, disturbing nature as little as possible. Nature itself—Mother Nature, we would say—will show us herself how to live, if we but look and listen. Nature has a certain predictability, not because it is deterministic but because it follows typical patterns. It may or may not be cyclical, repeating itself over long time periods, though that was often the ancient and traditional view. That view has, interestingly, been revived by some arguing from quantum cosmology.

The modern nature religions are not so much opposed to history as bored by it. History is interesting if you are interested in it, but it is not important. Human action in a naturalistic world is a product of nature. It was never exhaustively deterministic in any practical sense, and it is impossible for it to be deterministic even in theory; quantum mechanics tells us that much. The problem is not so much about natural causes as about how we narrate human actions. In one style of narrative (the biblical heritage), human actors can answer for their actions; in another (the nature religions), they cannot, because nature itself is the real actor. Nature knows a few life-stories—archetypes, in the ancient versions of this way of living. In some modern versions, the archetypes are gone, and actions are decided on a day-to-day basis by neurophysiology or psychology. Yet the archetypes are very much alive and well, and great moneymakers in Hollywood.

Nature religion was identified as "polytheism" because it has many sources of meaning in life, without much overarching unity. The gods of nature affirm life in this world only when they bring gratification. They don't act for good in the pains of life, and so there is no very good way to integrate them into a coherent whole in a world where pain remains. One response to the pains of life in the Greco-Roman world was Stoicism. Gnosticisms were another.

Some examples of contemporary nature religions: the Wiccan revival; deep ecology; environmentalism; evolution as basic life orientation and ultimate meaning in life; quantum cosmology as human cosmology also; Freudian psychology; Jungian psychology. Actually, almost any kind of psychology as determinative of human action qualifies as a naturalistic life orientation. Many of these can be adopted in varying degrees: evolution accepted as science does not compel one to turn evolution into the ultimate meaning of human life. Care for the environment does not compel one to embrace environmentalism as a religion-substitute, though some do.

Biblical religion, world-affirming historical religion, the (2) of section 5.6, we defer to the following sections.

Exilic religion, the ancient gnosticisms, (3) of section 5.6, p. 101, would seem not to have modern analogs, apart from a tiny revival and its following among academics. Some (e. g. Eric Voegelin) find mutated versions of it in totalitarian politics, Marxism especially, but that story is too long for us.

The meditative traditions always offer solace and a way out of the pains of life for those who don't find nature particularly helpful and are not interested in the rigors of biblical religion. This is (4) in the ancient world, p. 102.

Turning politics into a religion is easy: all you have to do is not look beyond politics, not allow any criticism of your chosen politics, and make your politics the ultimate meaning in life. This is a modern analog of (5), p. 102. Examples are too numerous, too obvious, and too contentious to recount. What goes for politics goes for class warfare also. Some versions (Marxisms, socialisms) have elaborate theory, but this is something that can, in a pinch, be done without theory.

"New Age Mysticism" is the analog of the ancient mystery religions, (6) on p. 102. Every kind of self-help, get-ahead, and therapy program known to man is available today.

Many people don't much need "religion" today; for them, informalism and secularism are quite sufficient. This is the (7) of section 5.6, p. 102. Such people can get through life without theory, without specialists, without intentional remedies. This is much like ancient Hellenistic culture, as Luther Martin well showed. When he took his students through the Hellenistic world, they were fascinated because it offered so many parallels to contemporary society. If informalism is not adequate, there are modern mystery religions.

The Hellenistic world is notable for the popularity of religions imported from exotic cultures in Asia. Our age is like that. Islam and Asian religions are available in America in every large city.

8.2 Biblical Choices

Biblical religion in the West today lives with the widespread but far from universal failure of the modern supernatural as a mode of transcendence, a way of access to God. That is old—but not finished—news. Those who reject transcendence by way of violations of laws of nature *and those who still accept that model of transcendence* live with this cultural condition.

Rabbinic Judaism has, on the whole, dealt with these problems much better than has Christianity. Since I am a Christian and the problems are mostly in the Christian form of biblical religion, let me record my respect for the other Exodus tradition, and concentrate on where the problems are.

The menu of options in Christianity in America today is pretty well known and not very surprising, so the summary in this section will be brief. The stereotypes put Fundamentalists (and with them, Ultramontanists) on one end and Liberal theology on the other. In the middle are too many theologies to catalog usefully, and readers generally know their way around well enough anyway. A student in Berkeley once found over a hundred different kinds of Evangelicals, and Evangelicals are hardly the only theologies in the "middle." That is where my heart lies, but my goal here is not to side with some against others. After some observations about the Fundamentalists and Liberals, I would like to emphasize once again a little of what modern biblical criticism and contemporary philosophical resources offer to theology in the middle. Most of it we have seen already.

Many Fundamentalists (and not a few Ultramontanists) could not be very comfortable with what I have said in this book. Nevertheless, it is not my intent to demonize Fundamentalists. We can occasionally pray together, even if we cannot easily do theology together. In particular, I would like to acknowledge the hospitality of the Grand Rapids Reformed Baptist congregation, on numerous visits with my family in the area; a hospitality especially gracious since I am Roman

Catholic. What goes for Fundamentalists goes, with appropriate modifications and fewer disagreements, for ultra-conservative Catholics. I would happily trust my life to Fundamentalists and Ultramontanists, staunchly pro-life all, as I could not without great risk among Liberals.

Credit is due to the traditions that are broadly called "liberal" (little "l," including most theologies in the middle and even some Ultramontanists) for accepting modern biblical criticism. Indeed "liberals" originated modern biblical criticism, with great courage and at great risk (p. 12 above). That having been said, there are many problems in the specific tradition that traces its lineage back to Friedrich Schleiermacher, the father of Liberal Theology. It tends to be Marcionite: Beyond its convenient use as a weapon in class warfare, the Old Testament is not much used in theology, even if it is required of seminarians. The high-water mark of Marcionite theology was probably a hundred years ago, with Adolf Harnack, the dean of Liberal Theology in his day. He candidly said the Old Testament ceased to be necessary by the time of the Reformation, and is utterly useless today. Jesus is the focus, but Jesus is merely a teacher, a good example. Jesus had more "God-consciousness" than you or I do, but we can follow in his footsteps. What Jesus *did* doesn't make much difference today—beyond his good example. The road back has been through Neo-Orthodox theology and the reforms of Vatican II: the Protestant scholars rediscovered how important the Exodus is, and Vatican II restored the requirement of actually reading it in the Sunday liturgy.

The reactionary rejection of modern biblical criticism is well known. Liberal theology and Fundamentalism feed on each other, because each has legitimate complaints about necessary parts of a vital theology that are missing in the other's program. The traffic between them has been somewhat bitter. Yet they share too many common assumptions. Neither has a viable sense of the transcendence of God: transcendence in Fundamentalism is by means of the modern supernatural, which doesn't work very well, and transcendence is largely missing in Liberal theology. Fundamentalism reads the Gospels as factual accounts of exactly what Jesus said and did. In a grotesque parody, the (very Liberal) Jesus Seminar has published a four-color text of the Gospels, with Jesus' words in different colors from red to pink to gray to black, just like the old Fundamentalist red-letter Gospels, (which had only red for Jesus' words, without any doubts). The Jesus Seminar thinks it can tell which sayings are authentic and which are from later editors. Neither Fundamentalists nor (on this point) the Jesus Seminar realize that the Bible is the Church's book, written by the Church, for the Church's purposes. The Church is older than the Bible, the Church has authority over the Bible, not the other way around. One perverse modern assumption underlying this mistake is sometimes called "historicism," the idea that it is even possible to recover a history that is "exactly" what happened. That was an ambition of nineteenth-century German scholars, and in the end, they knew they were beaten. We can know a great deal about the past, but rarely can we know "exactly" what happened in any detail.

Liberal theology accepts critical history, but it undermines transcendence. Liberal theology was right to give up the modern supernatural, which doesn't really work. But with nothing to replace it, the move was a leap of faith without much to land on. It undermines transcendence utterly.

To their credit, both Liberal and Fundamentalist Christians sometimes rise above the problems with their explanations of transcendence, and just proceed with colloquial language about God. Somehow it all works out and they muddle through, which is about as well as can be expected of anyone. To paraphrase the words of H. Richard Niebuhr, they, like all Christians, see God as acting in all actions on them, and try to respond always so as to respond to Him (*The Responsible Self*, p. 126).

The problem is about transcendence, and we shall focus on it in sections 8.3 and 8.4. Transcendence is a philosophical problem, yet both Liberal Theology and Fundamentalism think they can do theology without any support from philosophy. Nevertheless, bad theory or lack of theory can undermine or corrupt practice. If you don't have a way to talk about transcendence, it is all too easy to give up the things that only transcendence can do for you, and theology becomes impoverished. A playful acquaintance once inflicted on her father, a priest, the spoonerism that "Christ our Sackover has been pacified for us." It garbles the invitation to Communion in the 1979 *Book of Common Prayer*, "Christ our Passover has been sacrificed for us." (The priest was understandably terrified he would inadvertently inflict his daughter's spoonerism on a congregation during a mass.) Whatever a "sackover" is, it is not the costly difference-making sacrifice that the Passion used to be. And the challenge of the Gospel has been pacified: "A God without wrath brought men without sin into a kingdom without judgment through the ministrations of a Christ without a cross," in H. Richard Niebuhr's appraisal of Liberal Theology in *The Kingdom of God in America* (p. 193). This is what happens with deferred maintenance of philosophical explanations of transcendence. With neglect of philosophy and consequent atrophy of transcendence, Liberal theology had little to offer but what is more easily available as secular politics and therapy.

For a Catholic, I have depended disproportionately on Protestant sources for biblical scholarship, so I hope my criticisms in a Catholic vein will not be taken as unduly partisan. Both Fundamentalism and Liberal theology are of Protestant origin. It has, by contrast, been a Catholic tradition that the theologian has some responsibilities in philosophy that may not be shirked. That virtue has usually been practiced to excess by Catholics, for in Catholic tradition, theology starts with philosophy and philosophy ignores the Bible. Something in the middle should be possible, seeking responsible philosophical explanations of what it means to continue the biblical tradition today. It will not be easy. Perhaps the Catholic duty of philosophical responsibility can be made palatable by observing that many of the philosophical resources are Protestant. On the other side, Catholic biblical scholarship has pretty much recovered from the disabilities imposed under Pius X. It has amply caught up with Protestant scholarship.

One way of trying to discharge the philosophical obligations goes by the name of "science and religion," on the assumption that the modern challenges to Christianity come from science, and if we can show that science and religion are compatible, or better still, that the claims of theology can be given some underlying support from science, then the problems will be solved. I don't think it works that way. In the first place, as we have seen, the "problems" between science and religion all arise from the mistake of trying to explain theology in the terms of science in the first place: that is where the modern supernatural came from in the seventeenth century (section 6.6). The problems for theology come from history, relativity, and pluralism, not from science.

It is not true, by the way, that science and theology have nothing to say to each other; merely that *this* approach will not be fruitful. The content of scientific theory sets some limits on what the theologian can say, though the limits are minimal and broad. The real locus of dialogue should be, on the scientific side, at the level of the *presuppositions* of the scientific endeavor, not the content of scientific theory. On the theological side, it should start with resources in Continental philosophy. (Heidegger, clear and easy in other areas, will be difficult here; he didn't much like science.) Too much of the English-speaking Analytic tradition in philosophy has continued as if Kant, Kierkegaard, and hermeneutics had never happened. For the foreseeable future, this problem will be technical and difficult. In any case, there is today little interest in such a conversation, and this book has more important problems to work on.

"Science and religion" tends to resuscitate strategies that were first tried in the eighteenth century. Scientists who are atheists are not convinced, as they should not be, though they can usually afford to ignore "science and religion." It is a big fish in the small pond of theology, but it is quite a small fish in the much bigger pond of culture at large.

Those who seek peace between science and religion in this strategy want peace on science's terms: The topic of central interest is nature, not history. It is as if they pray Psalm 104 (the glory of God in nature) but never get to Psalms 105 or 106 (about the Exodus and history). At this point, one might justifiably ask, "science and *which* religion?" Clearly not a religion of history.

Another variant of "science and religion," natural theology, has brought back arguments from nature to God. Such arguments are philosophically naive, and don't notice that the nature that is in the premises is considerably more than the nature of the natural sciences: The nature of the natural sciences knows nothing of values, ethics, suffering, the humanities, or transcendence, yet all of those have to be projected onto the nature of the sciences in order to insinuate them into the conclusions about God. The projections are philosophically undisciplined, unmethodical, uncriticized, unjustified, unconscious, and so unrecognized. Those who actually have dual competence at a professional level, in both the hard sciences and theology informed by Continental phenomenology, can easily recognize what is going on. George Pattison has characterized this approach (e. g., in John Polkinghorne) as an extremely sophisticated revival of Paley's strategy (Pattison, p. 21, n. 14).

In yet another variant, "science and religion" is still looking for ways to have volokinesis, without interfering with laws of nature. This is the purpose of locating acts of God in the indeterminacy of quantum mechanics. Sometimes people even fall back on violations of laws of nature, so long as God is tactful and discreet about it, and doesn't do it where scientists can watch it happen. (That would be Creationism, and it would cause problems with science.)

With these long preliminaries aside, let's review what we've learned about biblical religion in the course of its history. It is *about* history—and about covenant. Covenant is the commitment that God will in some sense provide good in the vicissitudes of life, however painful. More of that in a moment.

The Exodus was a move from nature to history. It was not really consolidated until late in Second Temple Judaism. I don't think the move can ever be finally closed, because history itself is unpredictable and culture will change in unforeseeable ways forever. We will always be discovering new ways to live in history, because the problems of living in history will never stop changing.

Merold Westphal observed that nature is the prolog to history, not its model. It is just the stage on which history plays out. Nature is today the nature of the natural sciences, and in that sense, the sciences set some limits on what theology can do. But just as Sophocles can be performed on a modern stage as well as in an ancient Greek theater, the changes in the natural world usually don't force radical changes in how theology is done. The *theology* in Genesis 1–2, even though it is set in a world long gone, still works today even though the *cosmology* of Genesis 1–2 is bizarre.

Nature may be the stage for history, but it does not determine the drama that is performed on that stage. In a nature religion, nature is the model for human life ever after, and so the nature of the natural sciences assumes a much more important role in religion. In a nature religion, nature determines what people do. In historical religion, nature does not determine what human beings do. In historical religion, you are responsible for your actions, which is to say that as a member in a historical community, you are jointly responsible for telling what has happened and for criticizing the narratives you tell, and so also for criticizing the acts you tell stories about.

Mircea Eliade observed that history is disorder, chaos, unpredictability, and all too often suffering and affliction in the bargain. Taken raw, history is intolerable. The pain is too great. Nature at least provided some predictable meaning in life, when human values could be surreptitiously projected onto nature. Nature so understood was hospitable to human life. When those projections don't work, or become visible, or history intrudes, there is a problem. A historical religion won't work without something like covenant: the trust that ultimate reality will somehow provide good even in the pains and disorder of history. The Hebrews complained to Moses, as we have seen, in the Exodus: "will God be *with* us, or not? We can't see him." That is the problem of transcendence.

Parallels between the Exodus and the Gospels usually don't get central attention in New Testament courses today. I think that is a shame, because the parallels are central: the Exodus shapes the Gospels, as we saw in section 7.5. The message of the Gospels is that what God did for you before (twice, in the Exodus and the Exile), God is doing for you again in Jesus and the Disasters of the First Century. That message challenges and invites, but it offers no proof or demonstration. The stance of the believer is accordingly somewhat precarious: he has no response to those who would refuse the invitation, defy the challenge. He is at some risk, and the problem of risk comes next, in dealing with what are called "sacred canopies."

8.3 Sacred Canopies

A good part of the religious desolation in the modern world came from the loss of taken-for-granted certainty that the Christian universe used to have. Earlier, it seemed as if anything other than the Christian cosmos was unthinkable. In the modern world other possibilities became quite thinkable, and quite choosable, thereby exposing Christianity as a choice, not something necessary. All the religious options of section 5.6 came flooding back, sometimes recognized, sometimes not.

The religious desolation of the modern world comes not from the loss of God but from the loss of a what Peter Berger called a "sacred canopy." A sacred canopy is a conceptual world that is designed to protect its inhabitants from anxiety. Anxiety comes from lack of certainty, the possibility of chaos and meaninglessness in the cosmos, the apparent absence of God, and in general, the fragility and precariousness of the world as religion views it. Anxiety comes from hecklers, outsiders who think your religion is bunk. And anxiety comes, deep down, from self-doubt, much of which is healthy and necessary. Liberal Theology, by the way, for all my complaints about it on other grounds, has generally been pretty good about living without a sacred canopy.

The religious desolation of the modern world comes more particularly from not recognizing our lot as something that should be familiar: it is the same desolation that the Hebrews faced in the wilderness, in the Exodus. If people today could recognize that, they could say, "We've been here before, and even though we were lost then, too, the Lord was with us, even though he didn't seem to be. We should know how to deal with this. It's religious home for us." It is also hard work. The cosmos that results is precarious.

The problems of religion in the West today are more like biblical times than the medieval and modern periods: We experience our religious choices *as* choices, not as a necessary world that is objective, unchangeable, and can be taken for granted. The necessity of choice is quite obvious in Joshua 23–24, the covenant renewal ceremony, and that ritual choosing was only one of many, even in the Bible. Apparently it was a regular liturgy.

Whatever may be said about the Exodus itself, the Exodus *texts* were edited at a much later date, during the monarchy, when Israelite society was relatively stable and secure. So it is not necessary to have social instability to appreciate the fundamental anxiety and precariousness of this kind of religion. In final form the texts were edited when Israel had fallen and Judah was soon to fall (or recently fallen), so there was anxiety enough in the air. The editors turned to the Exodus tradition to strengthen them in their hour of need: "we've been through this anxiety before, we can do it again." The Lord is present, even in his apparent absence. That lesson would help us today.

For whatever reason, medieval Christianity experienced itself differently, and whether it knew it or not, set about to construct a sacred canopy. It took the form of devising proofs of the existence of God, a tradition that continues in some quarters into the present. But people who believe proofs of God always believe *in* proofs of God, because they have to believe the premises of the proofs (something other than God) more than, or before, the conclusion (God). Otherwise, why would anyone want proofs at all? A proof is perfect for a sacred canopy: it takes the responsibility of faith, so the believer doesn't have to. A proof makes it look like the religion proven has to be right, and could not *not* be right.

Some who would defend proofs of God (and with them the sacred canopy the proofs support) accuse proof-deniers of "fideism." Fideism is an "attitude of mind" that denies "the power of unaided human reason to reach certitude" about the existence of God (*Catholic Encyclopedia*, "Fideism," New Advent website, 2007-06-22). Unaided here means unaided by faith or revelation. The problem is posed in quite medieval terms. The trouble is, one cannot come to believe in the Lord of History without knowing something about history. History properly understood is revelation: Revelation is effectively the history that makes sense of the rest of history and gives meaning to life (H. Richard Niebuhr, *The Meaning of Revelation*). The anti-fideists tell us that reason unaided by knowledge of history can reach the God of history? The God proposed for belief cannot be the biblical God.

To call someone a fideist is to call him irresponsible, to accuse him of shirking a philosophical obligation. The insinuation is that the fideist's faith is based on authority, or worse, on caprice and whimsy. I don't think so. Unless you can say of those in biblical religion, whether in life or literature, "I want what they have," you really shouldn't be getting into biblical religion at all. Saying "I want what they have" presupposes knowing something of what it means to do a world-affirming historical religion, so such a choice is not made without knowledge.

This book does not advocate fideism, it assumes a confessional method in theology. To call another a fideist is a charge of irresponsibility, but charges of fideism cover up a deeper irresponsibility on the part of the accusers: The quest for "objective" proofs of the basis of faith. That quest is an evasion of responsibility, of the responsibilities incumbent on any who would confess biblical faith.

Perhaps the anxiety of giving up a sacred canopy can be palliated a little in this way: To give up certainty is uncomfortable. The implication is that we could be wrong. Something stronger can be said, merely from experience and the trust that the future will be like the past: From time to time, we *will* be wrong. The response of faith is to trust that events will show us up as wrong (exposure): we will not be left in our errors, wrong though we do not know it. Events themselves (limitation) will bring the remedies, in an opening to creativity, especially when we share our troubles with one another (need). The future will indeed be like the past: exposure, limitation, and need will come, and they will bring grace and blessings.

8.4 The Problem of God

The problem with transcendence is that it cannot be demonstrated. Some things in this world give rise to unanswerable questions, and those questions point to transcendence. Those questions can simply be dismissed as meaningless by people who don't want to face them, and they can be answered in many ways, even by those who do face them. Not all answers come from world-affirming historical religion.

Some examples of unanswerable questions: Why is there a world at all, and not nothing? Why me? Why suffering? Why is the universe orderly and knowable as nature (this is the beginning of science)? To ask why is to ask for a place in a world that makes sense. "Boundary situations" are where the questioning stops (or perhaps starts); places where there are no more answers.

There is no way to justify responding to boundary situations with faith in something transcendent. It always remains a choice. Transcendence is, in any case, by definition invisible, not demonstrable. Belief in transcendence can accordingly be somewhat lonely. It is especially lonely if people around you don't share your belief.

This is not new: we saw this in the Exodus, when the Israelites cried out to Moses, "were there not graves enough in Egypt, that you had to bring us out here into the desert, to die? Where is the Lord when we need him?" (p. 61 above). Are we alone? The answer to Moses' question at the burning bush was not reassuring: Put one foot in front of the other, and don't worry about who I am. I will be with you as who I am. You will not see me, but I will be there. Now get moving.

It is especially galling when the neighbors heckle, "Where, now, O Israel, is your God?" There is nothing to point to. Today, people don't use the language they did three thousand years ago, "where, now," etc. Today they accuse you of what they are pleased to call "subjectivism," on the assumption that you should have something objective to point to. (This is a little like the complaining about "fideism" that we saw on p. 172.) What would please the objectors would be something "objective." And not all the objectors are today (or were, back then) on the outside. The worst are well within the fold of biblical religion. In their quest for something "objective," no less than the high priest, Aaron himself, built them a golden calf. And modern golden calves abound, in philosophical theories of religion designed to "prove" the existence of God or the truth of Christianity.

So what can you see and what is always a matter of faith in acts of God? What you can see are exposure, limitation, and need, in the cases where acts of God hurt, the cases that occupy most of our attention. You can even see, to some extent, how those pains of life get turned into good, how the goods of life come when least expected. To some extent: not everybody agrees about what *good* is. What you cannot *see* is that goods come *from God*. The divine character of acts of God is a matter of faith; the visible results of acts of God are of course quite visible, even to those who disagree about whether they bring good or not. Assuming for the moment the historicity of the Exodus texts about the parting of the Sea of Reeds, you can see the parting of the Sea, but you cannot see "objectively" whether it is an act of God or just an accident of the weather. To claim that God tampered with the weather where no scientist can see him do it (e. g., in quantum indeterminacy in the chaotic antecedents of the weather) does not really qualify as "objective": If no one can see it, what's the purpose of the claim? And why should we believe such a claim? That kind of "objectivity" comforts those who have invented it, though they cannot see why it is not convincing to those who don't need it or don't believe it.

These remarks about transcendence are barely more than hints. When I dealt with the problem all too briefly in chapter 5 of *Unwelcome Good News*, it still took many pages. Yet it can be said that those who are willing to live without proof, those who are willing to let God be invisible can enjoy transcendence and the presence of God easily enough today. To do that, you have to have some confidence that exposure, limitation, and need really do bring blessings, even when we cannot (or cannot yet) see those blessings, even when we are destroyed by exposure, limitation, and need, as we always are, in the end. That's the real issue, isn't it? Whether the pains of life bring blessings? If you believe they do, then transcendence is relatively easy; if you don't believe they do, this kind of transcendence is irrelevant.

Chapter 9

Christianity Today

9.1 Living in History

When beginning seminarians caricature their bible professors' approach as "First, we destroy your faith," they complain because critical history and critical biblical scholarship have *exposed* them and their faith as wanting. The appearance is much worse, that their alleged faith is based on a history that is erroneous and possibly downright fraudulent. I hope the argument of this book has shown that the reality is quite different from that appearance. Biblical history was a history of faith, a history that is still viable in the present. We can continue what they did.

We saw the companions of history at the outset, in section 1.3; they are relativity and pluralism. Limitation appears as historical and cultural relativity, and need appears as religious pluralism, religious disagreement. History, relativity, and pluralism are the real challenge, once the red herring of "science and religion" is out of the way. If history, relativity, and pluralism are seen as instances of exposure, limitation, and need, they can be appropriated as openings to grace.

The challenge of history can be evaded, blunted, turned or tamed in many ways. You can do that even while appearing to be a part of historical religion, by turning Jesus into a way to get out of the risks and dangers of history, instead of hearing Jesus as God come to be with us in those same dangers of history. The craving for ahistorical absolutes will always be with us. Yet we tolerate historical relativity in the sciences with supreme confidence, trusting that change in science brings good and progress. So why, if we can do that in science, is it so hard in historical religion?

Those who do historical religion and examine their own history critically stand in a tradition that has a long history, going back well into biblical texts. Those who would use critical history as a way of exposing historical religion for purposes hostile to historical religion are using tools they dare not turn on themselves, tools that are not their own, tools that belong to the historical religion they rebel against. The most the critics can accuse historical religion of is hypocrisy: not living up to its own standards. Inasmuch as critical history is a species of exposure, and exposure, limitation, and need are the face of God active in the world, critical history belongs to historical religion by birthright.

Relativity does not mean anything goes and nothing matters, it means that relative to your own time and place, you *can* tell what's right and what's wrong, and you don't need ahistorical absolutes valid for every conceivable and inconceivable culture in the future. The way of relativity is tradition-bound rationality: when one tradition can explain another's successes and failures better than the other itself can, the first is probably the better option. Alasdair MacIntyre showed this in the 1980s, and he deserves credit for solving a problem that stumped philosophers for centuries before.

Pluralism does not mean that all religions are equally valid, or that Christianity should just amalgamate with other religions. It tells us that all human beings are equally loved by God, and all have needs for meaning in life. All alike stand before the chaos and meaninglessness of the universe that is the face of holiness. Properly understood, religious pluralism is the basis for evangelism, not the end of evangelism, but it is the basis for evangelism that respects the cultures and religious traditions in which it evangelizes, rather than simply trying to abolish them. The presupposition of history, relativity, and pluralism, after all, was prior experience of embracing exposure, limitation, and need as bearing blessings in history. It would be incoherent to give up historical religion on the basis of historical religion—which is what syncretism with nature religions or exilic religions would be.

The watershed in the history of religions was the Exodus, not the Disasters of the First Century. This is so even though the Exodus can't be recovered as an event. We saw as much in the analogy of crossing the Continental Divide on the interstate highway in southern Wyoming, in sections 3.5 and 4.3.

One of the major themes when we came to the New Testament was Exodus typology, the Exodus as model for the Gospels. This is not the "traditional" way of reading the Gospels, despite the fact that it appears to be the way the Gospels were actually written. The traditional reading is to project Jesus back into the Common Documents, reading the prophets as predictions of Jesus and the history as foreshadowing Jesus. I always had to work to get my Old Testament students not to do that, out of respect for the integrity of the Common Documents that we inherit along with the Synagogue. They learned quite easily, once they saw the right way to relate the two testaments: not by projecting Jesus onto the Common Documents, but projecting the Exodus onto the life of Jesus. That's what the Gospel writers did: they used the Exodus (already familiar) to interpret the life and death of Jesus (not yet making sense). The difference is important: it is the difference between Exodus typology and a quasi-Marcionite theology. Not fully Marcionite; the tradition still reads the Old Testament. But the tradition made disastrous concessions to Marcion in the very act of repudiating his theology: it made the primary testament secondary, a mere prologue. The Common Documents were (and are) the foundation.

The message of the Gospels is that what God did for you before, he is doing for you again today. The "before" is more important than the "again, today," since the latter is (or was, in the first century) harder to understand, harder to make sense of. The message in this book is very similar: what God did for you before, he is doing for you again today. He came to you in exposure, limitation, and need, and he is doing that again, specifically in history, relativity, and pluralism.

One of the lessons from history is that the covenant people has a responsible liberty of interpretation in choices about how it wants to conduct the covenant. Liberal Theology tends to be deaf to responsibility, and Fundamentalism deaf to the liberty. We should be able to see the responsible liberty of interpretation, just from the history. One part of first-century Judaism chose to interpret the Jesus events in terms of the Exodus, and another did not, preferring to emphasize the law, which it proceeded to systematize in the Mishnah. The survivors dealt creatively with the loss of the Temple. Other groups in first-century Judaism did not survive at all.

The Church and the Synagogue still have to learn to live with each other, neither trying to disinherit the other from the promises of the Exodus and Second Temple Judaism. That problem is not yet solved. As usual, rabbinic Judaism is ahead of the Church. But this much can be said, at least from the Christian side: The Church needs the Synagogue to be strong, healthy, and different. In its difference, it exposes the Church as creaturely, as a covenantal people exercising its responsible liberty of interpretation, simply by exercising that same liberty differently. Not all exposure is exposure of sin. But he who exposes me discharges for me the office of Christ, and the Church should accordingly treat the Synagogue with the special respect, honor, and affection that derive from a shared inheritance in the Common Documents. Were that done, we would see the last of anti-Jewish theology in the Church and the last of anti-semitism in culture.

9.2 The Santa Claus Problem

A pastor's lot is not an easy one. A sermon affords only fifteen minutes once a week, people don't come regularly, they don't do assigned reading, they misunderstand, get alarmed, take offense and then blame it all on the pastor. And there are many other things that need preaching about besides critical history. So how is he to bring his parishioners through the thrills and anxieties of learning how the Bible was put together? Even in schools, where there is cooperation from students, teachers tackle the problem very gingerly. Telling people that the actual history was not always what the Bible appears to say is too much like explaining to your older kids that there is no Santa Claus, but there really is a Santa Claus, if you take my meaning. One does that when the younger kids are not around, and takes the older kids into parental confidence, trusting that they will not spoil it for the younger ones.

This is the Santa Claus problem in religious education. It is connected to the problem of sacred canopies; what protects the young and popular religion from unbearable dread (and is not really a guilty sacred canopy) becomes (at the adult stage, at least) what is indeed a sacred canopy, functioning to protect people who should know better from contact with real religious risk, and so to protect them from contact with the holiness of God.

The Santa Claus problem cannot be solved just by pitching explanations to the lowest level, to beginners in faith, to the most naive. To do that betrays and deprives those who are capable of understanding biblical history without being upset by it. Many of those people learn outside the Church to reject literal interpretations of the Bible, and then they leave the faith entirely. Yet if the unsophisticated hear the same biblical criticism, they will conclude that biblical religion is bunk, and they, too, will leave. Offering a real message of good news in biblical terms to both groups is exquisitely delicate. (And disagreeing with Fundamentalists without demonizing them is equally delicate.)

I once saw credited to Paul Tillich the insight that naiveté has its rights and its privileges: the sophisticated or post-naive have no right to break up other people's naiveté. Yet when that naiveté breaks up on its own, it has to be helped. You can't just abandon people whose naiveté has been shattered. And even the naive do not have a right to protect their own naiveté by obstructing the education of those for whom naiveté no longer works.

The coordinator for preparation of adults for baptism in my parish once said, more or less to me, knowing that I am a theologian familiar with biblical criticism, "Do not teach us things we will have to unlearn later. Do not teach us things that are wrong. Do not teach us things you will have to un-teach us later." But we do that in physics all the time! So why is it so hard in catechesis, when people take it in physics "like a child upon its mother's breast," with a soul that "is quieted within me"?

The sciences handle the problem with ease: beginning students learn Newtonian classical physics. Later they have to learn that what they learned earlier was wrong—twice! Once from relativistic physics, and once from quantum mechanics. Why is it so easy in physics, and so hard with the Bible? Why is it so hard when we correct naive literal interpretations of the Bible with "JEDP and all that," and then say that scholars have doubts about the J and E parts, and much of the timing and editing? When older theories in the sciences are modified by newer theories, people rejoice and call it progress. When received interpretations in biblical religion are shown to need modification, people think life has no meaning. Why is historical relativity handled with ease in the natural sciences, but not in historical religion?

There is a deep irony here: We are comfortable living with the unknown and with unanswered questions in the sciences, but you can get yourself lynched for heresy if you try to suggest that we might also do that in "religion." The irony is that however much history figures in science's communal disputes, history never appears in scientific explanations, which are utterly naturalistic. But a supposedly historical religion is today making heavy weather of historical explanations of its own past, and having an even rougher time dealing with change in doctrine and unanswered questions in theology.

Our time is one of caution about explanations of how the past happened. We began with the documentary hypothesis, on p. 24 and in section 3.3, and followed the hypothesis in its simple form through chapters 3 and 4. The details have never commanded universal agreement, but the general shape of the hypothesis withstands critics, even if it cannot be refined to give the precise textual history that we would so crave.

The technical arguments don't matter here so much as the popular instinctive response to them. Many responded with horror to the original documentary hypothesis, because it seemed to make the texts less divine or less authoritative. News of problems with it can only bring joy to their instincts. I think that is a misreading of the implications of biblical scholarship.

Before the documentary hypothesis, the Bible was simply the Word of God, in the sense that we could take it as God speaking to us, *simply*. God's Word is God's words, and we don't have to worry about its origins or about human responsibility for the texts. We can trust it just as it is. Or something like that.

This instinct is partly right and partly wrong. Where it is right, it has never been well explained. Where it is wrong, it stonewalls and evades responsibility for the human origins of the texts. That kind of denial and evasion we have seen already, in sacred canopies.

There are two problems with the documentary hypothesis, even if it is assumed to be right. The first and lesser hazard is that it can be turned into yet another sacred canopy, providing a new certainty to replace the old, pre-critical certainty. It can thus be used to protect believers from the anxieties of belief. I think many in the nineteenth century wanted their historians to produce just such a certainty. They called it "scientific" history, because it was supposed to produce "objective" results, just like the natural sciences. That quest failed, and its failure is widely acknowledged today.

In the second place, the documentary hypothesis is recent (only 150 years old), and if it is to provide saving knowledge of history, it can only save those who know about it, and even they are not many among the faithful today. All the others' faith is then in vain, because they don't know the documentary hypothesis. Clearly this will not work: you are supposed to believe in God and the acts of God in history, not necessarily in this version of history. Sorting that out is more complicated than I know how to do, but some things can be said.

Saving *knowledge* is not quite what we are looking for; such would be better for gnosticisms, in which salvation really does come from knowledge. That having been said, biblical religion is based on its history, and some sort of knowledge of history is necessary, even if it is not the precise knowledge so prized by scholars. Throughout the long career of biblical religion, believers have never put their faith in academic accuracy. Colloquial knowledge of history has been fairly loose and informal, and that informal relating to history has sufficed quite well. It has sent countless saints to the Heavenly Banquet.

As it happens, there are witnesses to this even among academics. Some years ago, a series of meditations on the Sunday readings was published as *The Gospel in Solentiname* (Ernesto Cardenal), about how rural Nicaraguans understand the gospels without benefit of higher criticism. Academics know that lay people don't need academics in order to believe or be saved, and they are somewhat puzzled by their own irrelevance. This insight was never pushed very far, and it became quite hypocritical (this is an American thing) when it refused to recognize that American Fundamentalists and Evangelicals have the same ability as Nicaraguan laity to believe without help from academics.

Sometimes scholars do better than this. Yosef Haim Yerushalmi pointed out that Jewish believers over the centuries have never relied on academic scholarship. He is a professional historian at Columbia, and has devoted his working life to critical history and all its controversies and uncertainties and skepticism. But the Bible commands us to remember—Zakhor!—as the Hebrew has it. It doesn't tell us to do critical history. It didn't know critical history. Why remember? It is an obligation of gratitude: "I'm the one who brought you out of Egypt, but you forgot, and forgetting, you were ungrateful, and ungrateful, you were nasty to your neighbors." That's about what Amos says (2:6–16). It's what the Short Historical Creed says in Deuteronomy 26 (p. 154 above). You have an obligation to remember how you came to enjoy your blessings—material blessings, to be sure, but more importantly, the religious blessings of knowing how to live in all the uncertainties and perils of history.

Note that Amos's reproach is directed only to Israel—the obligation to remember is only for those doing a historical religion. The surrounding kingdoms had no such obligation, because they were not party to a Covenant. (Why he leaves out Judah is unclear to me; but perhaps merely because the message was directed to Israel.) Damascus, Gaza, Tyre, Edom, Ammon, and Moab were not told to remember, though they are condemned for their atrocities anyway, covenant or no.

Yerushalmi tells a little about how Jews remember. Among Catholics (closer to home, for me) it is usually by exercises such as the mysteries of the Rosary. Actually reading the Bible might be too radical. But for what it is worth, those few Episcopalians who do the Daily Office readings from the Lectionary soon end up with a remarkable knowledge of scripture. Others can do that, too, and the Prayer Book is not the only place to find a lectionary. It was my experience that merely reading the Bible is not enough: many things don't make very good sense without technical help, but that is easily available.

How can I have an obligation to know history—to remember, as the command has it—if the history available to me is fragmentary and full of errors, and if I don't study very hard? This question silently presupposes that certainty is required, that only certain knowledge saves, and that errors or gaps leave us abandoned, thrown out of covenant. When we worked through exposure, limitation, and need, and worked through how they come to us in critical history, cultural relativity, and religious pluralism, we saw that certainty is not required. Exposure will come—in the form of critical history—and correct whatever mistakes my own time makes. It is exposure that saves (pp. 6 and 158 above). When it comes as critical history, the word gets out, eventually, from universities to schools and the clergy, and then to ordinary people. We live with uncertainty in the sciences, and so it is just a little bit ridiculous to demand certainty in "religion." We believe in science, but that does not mean we all have to be scientists. We can believe in the blessings that come from history, but that does not mean that everybody has to be a critical historian.

9.3 Jesus in Bakersfield

We began with a radio evangelist who was a bit transparent in his arrangement of the "healings" of the hired shills on stage for his live audience. But apart from questions of integrity, is it any different in the Gospels? Mark does the same thing: There are thirteen identified people healed in the Gospel of Mark. They come in a series, as Edward Hobbs noticed. It starts with small body parts (here a hand, there a leg), and progresses to larger and larger things, culminating in whole-body healings. Interspersed among the healings are several feedings. Some healings are raisings, some are cleansings. The full list is in *Waters*, pp. 103–104.

After this series comes the cleansing of the Temple, the feeding of the disciples at the Last Supper, and the raising of Jesus, the Resurrection. There is a message here. Hobbs noticed that the sequence of "miracles" builds up to a climax. The little ones prepare you for the bigger ones, and the whole series prepares you for the three at the end. Edward Hobbs reads the miracle stories as TV advertisements, which are preposterous in order to make a point about the product they are selling. (He was not the only one; Gary Dreibelbis has seen this way of reading the miracle texts, too.)

The modern world tends to think that unless God interferes with the natural course of events, he doesn't "really" act in this world, as we saw in section 6.6. This is a legacy of the scientific world view, or better, of confusions that came with modern science. People instinctively think an act happens only when there is will-directed motion: human acts are motions directed by human willing, and divine acts are events directed by the divine will. And will makes things happen differently from how they would have happened otherwise.

This idea, taken to its apparent logical conclusion, thinks that will and consciousness are things other than human brain activity, and so they must have a way to influence what happens in the brain, since the brain stands in between will and the muscle motions that an act is all about. The reaction has been not just denial of any such supernatural (correctly, in my opinion), but also a denial that there is "anything there except brain activity." But where is this "there"? Consider an example. If I ask you what you want to eat tonight, I want to know what *you* want, not what your brain cells want. Your brain cells don't want at all, they just ooze neurotransmitters. There are a lot of them, and they are very complex, and a little is known about them in neurophysiology, but that is not how we understand wanting, choosing, and acting in everyday life. If you say "lets go out for sushi," I can interpret that response only because I know you, you have a history of food preferences, we live in a culture with culinary choices, a culture that stands as background for any choice such as this one. The background is part of the "there" every bit as much as the nerve activity in your brain. What gets included is a matter of editing, and of interpretation. What gets included determines what kind of act your response is. If we both know I hate raw fish, then your act is not a positive response at all, it is a case of "giving me a hard time." If I know that *you* hate raw fish, then your act is a case of "messing with my mind," not exactly the same kind of act.

To deny that there is anything "there" except brain activity is more than is needed to fend off the supernatural or the sorts of Platonist dualism that need such a supernatural. It also surreptitiously restricts the "there" to what's in the actor's brain. We don't do that in real life, not just because we can't see what's in somebody's brain, but because we *can* see what's going on in the lives of the people affected, and so we make sense of action in the context of what we know about those people and their world.

To talk about the brain as the "cause" of action is to focus on the natural and divert attention from the humanities, and from the processes of interpretation by which we make sense of acts. All of that is the realm of *narrative*. An act is anything that can be narrated, or perhaps act corresponds to the verbs in a narrative, and the actor is the implied subject of those verbs. Differential equations and theories about nerve dynamics are not narratives. A narrative is a story that has a problem, a goal, a plot, and some kind of solution to the problem and progress (or not) toward the goal—even if it is about something as elementary as tying your shoes. None of those elements of narrative can come from the sciences, even though everything the story talks about may have a completely natural substrate. The sciences cannot tell you *which* things belong in the story, or *why*. Another thing the sciences cannot handle is the case of acts of omission, for an act of omission presupposes that there are prior reasons to think engaging in the omitted act is relevant. Those prior reasons are not the sort of thing the natural sciences can provide; they come from narratives, and from the responsible editing of narratives; in a word, from human concerns.

If human acts cannot be understood by resources from the sciences alone, what about divine acts? If you look at the language and experience of acts of God, what you will find is *analogy* with human acts. That is, acts of God happen in the narratives we tell to make sense of our lives. It is a surprising and refreshing contrast to the will-directed motion theory. The opening joke about the man in a flood who wanted to be saved by a visible, certifiable act of God, who wouldn't accept God acting incognito, shows that we already know that volokinesis is the wrong way to think about acts of God.

So why do people typically respond to a theory of action like this with "so God doesn't *really* act, then?" What does "really" mean, here? It pretty clearly means volokinesis, will-directed motion: divine fiat directing what happens in this world, with divine fiat interpreted as a *physical* cause. It may be a fifth force, in addition to the four known to physics. It may be what resolves quantum indeterminacy, but it is still understood physically. And people who speak of "really acting" in this way also assume that if there is no physical aspect of divine action, no aspect explainable in naturalistic physical terms, then there can be no divine action. This, I think, is merely the visible face of something much more interesting. There are at least three issues in asking whether God "really" acts. (1) Do we really have blessings in the pains and limitations of life? (2) Are acts of God "objective"? (3) Is God *with* us, or are we alone? None of these are particularly simple, and some are quite subtle.

Do we have blessings in the pains of life? What would it mean to treat the pains of life as blessing-bearing? My solutions to the problem of pain were taken from Edward Hobbs: We trust that exposure of what we have been doing brings freedom from the past, a chance for repentance and amendment of life. We trust that the limitations of life bring opportunity, even if not what we would have preferred. We trust that encounter with others in need brings an opening to relatedness, community, fellowship.

About objectivity of acts of God: what would "objective" mean, here? Provable to other people who don't believe in God? I don't think either God or reality are offering that kind of proof. The Bible does not, though it is often mis-read to do just that. The Bible demands choice, commitment, trust, loyalty. You shall love the Lord your God with an undivided heart, with your whole person, and with all your involvements in the world. Proof is what would get you off the hook, excuse you from responsibility for your faith, your basic life orientation. If you are really committed in your basic life orientation, if you really know what you are doing, you don't need proof, you don't care about whether other people share your orientation to life or not. This is just the way things *are*, and those who don't see it that way are missing something. No proof is needed.

Is God *with* us, or are we alone? That's what the Hebrews asked Moses in the Exodus, complaining all the while. They wanted the comforts of objectivation in acts of God, and that's why they built the Golden Calf, which is pretty much where the quest for objectivity always ends up. God is not interested in giving objective proof. God wants commitment—from people who know what they are doing, who know they want to put a positive construction on all of life, even its hard and painful parts, because it's all in some sense, however painful, *good*. That's what "created" means.

The difference between Mark and the radio evangelist is that Mark takes acts of God in the meaning that insurance brokers give that phrase; the radio evangelist was playing to an audience who would take acts of God as interference with the natural. Actually, the radio evangelist is selling more than just interference with the natural. The radio evangelist is selling a way to get *out* of the pains of life, which is why he presumably needs interference with the natural course of events. Mark offers a way to find God's presence and blessing *in* the pains of life (which is the reason for the Passion narratives). Mark is selling reality; the radio evangelist is selling a way to get out of reality. If you want to put a positive construction on the world as it really is, then Mark may be for you.

The Holy Week Collects in the 1979 *Book of Common Prayer* understand: They ask, "grant that we, walking in the way of the cross, may find it none other that the way of life and peace"; "Grant us so to glory in the cross of Christ, that we may gladly suffer shame and loss for the sake of thy Son our Savior Jesus Christ"; "Give us grace to take joyfully the sufferings of the present time, in full assurance of the glory that shall be revealed." All three are modeled on an ancient collect for Palm Sunday: "Mercifully grant that we may walk in the way of his suffering, and also share in his resurrection." The message of Romans 8, the teaching of Jesus, and Bavli Berakhot 60b has been taken to heart: even in the pains of life lies the way to life more abundantly.

9.4 Not By the Wardrobe

In *The Lion, The Witch, and the Wardrobe*, four children from the Pevensie family are sent out of London during the blitz in World War II, to the country home of a professor Digory Kirk. There, taking refuge in a wardrobe to escape a housekeeper who is not sympathetic to them, they stumble into another world, Narnia. Actually, one of them, Lucy, gets in first, and Peter and Susan don't believe her. Edmund has been into Narnia with Lucy, but lies about it, betraying Lucy to the appearance of madness. Peter and Susan go to the professor for advice.

Digory Kirk appears only briefly in *The Lion, The Witch, and the Wardrobe* (he was the lead character in *The Magician's Nephew*, at the beginning of Narnia, but we do not know that). The professor's remarks are like the chorus in a Greek play, for he interprets the action for us. The scenes in Narnia, by far most of the book (and the movies) are what captivate readers and viewers, for that is where the Pevensie children discover a new reality and grow into it. It is in Narnia that Edmund is redeemed and the four meet Aslan, the figure of Christ in that world.

The scenes in England are quite brief, but they transact important business for C. S. Lewis. They are his quarrel with Oxford philosophers, and with their denial of transcendence. The question is about the reality of worlds "other" than this one. The BBC movie understood the professor's role well, and so understood that in this story, England is still the ordinary real world, where Narnia discloses what's real about it.

Peter and Susan ask the professor for advice on what to make of Lucy's preposterous stories about being in another world, Narnia.

We do not learn that the professor has himself been to Narnia. He is simply an old man offering sensible advice, the wisdom of years of experience. Having ruled out the possibilities that Lucy is lying or is mad, the only thing left is the possibility that she might be telling the truth. To Peter and Susan's disbelief in Lucy's report of another world, the professor replies, "That is more than I know." He disposes of a general principle that applies only some of the time, even in this world: real things are "there" all the time, for everybody, in the same way, no matter who looks at them. Indeed, that principle applies only in the natural sciences, and we are not in the world of the sciences, though that is not said. This is a story for children; I learned both to read and to believe from this book at about age six or seven.

Peter is dumbfounded. "But do you really mean, Sir, that there could be other worlds – all over the place, just round the corner—like that?"

"Nothing is more probable" is the professor's reply.

They adjourn without settling the matter, and a little later on, all four Pevensie children get into Narnia together, and the main action of the book commences. The adventures are cobbled together out of sixteenth-century ideas transformed in Lewis's vision; a world now lost to us, but real in the poetry of that century.

When it is all over, and they return to the professor's country house in England in 1940 via the wardrobe, They explain to the professor how four fur coats came to be missing from his wardrobe (it was winter in Narnia, and they needed the coats), and to their surprise, the professor believes their story entirely. Like the chorus in a drama, he sums up the action for the audience:

"I don't think it will be any good trying to go back through the wardrobe door to get the coats. You won't get into Narnia again by *that* route. ... don't go trying to use the same route twice. Indeed, don't *try* to get there at all. It'll happen when you're not looking for it."

Not by that route: This is our predicament today. We desperately want to get back to the pre-modern enchanted world when God, divine actions, the angels, heaven, and hell could be taken for granted. (Actually, that world is forgotten and very hard to recreate, even in scholarship; what we remember is the supernatural of the eighteenth century, not the enchanted world of the sixteenth.) That was our original naiveté, and it is gone, dissolved in the acids of modern historical scholarship and a worldview changed by the natural sciences. In truth, much of it was not very old, no older than the seventeenth century, the first century of modern science. Lewis sought refuge barely more than a century earlier, in the Aristotelian world that the 1600s spurned, a world where the virtues were alive in a cosmos that welcomed them, a world where people were at home. That being-at-home is called *primary naiveté*. We have not yet reached a secondary naiveté, one that is at home with the impossibility of the modern supernatural, yet simultaneously at home with the presence of transcendence in this world. We are not there yet.

The Platonist dualist supernatural that the academic establishment so despises in its sophistication will (with a little faith) get you to heaven, though it makes the foundations of modern science somewhat delicate, and though it hides some parts of the Bible rather completely. It doesn't recognize the Exodus, nor the transition from nature religions to historical religion, nor the radical challenge biblical religion makes to the world. It can't hear the liberty—and responsibility—of answering that is assumed in Jesus's question, "Who do you say that I am?" or Joshua's, "Which gods will you serve?"

We have not come to recognize the presence of acts of God all around us in a world that is more miraculous than we know (just as the two chemistry students wisecracked on their way up Highway 99 to Yosemite, but not in the way they thought). We are blind and deaf to acts of God. We cannot recognize the "miracle" stories as preposterous in a way we are familiar with from TV ads (p. 77), because we cannot recognize the product they are advertising.

The original doorway into transcendence was the time of Testing in the wilderness, the boundary situation that was the Exodus. C. S. Lewis didn't understand that, perhaps because he didn't understand even the biblical scholarship of his time, and much has happened since then. But the Exodus can again be for us a doorway into transcendence, because it marks the doorway from nature into history, and into trust that all of life, pains included, works for good for those who love the Lord, even in our precarious history.

Time Line

1200 BCE The Exodus: the date has never commanded universal agreement, and today scholars have diminished confidence that there was a single event that could be dated.

1000–961 The reign of David.

961–922 The reign of Solomon.

722 The Assyrians end the kingdom of Israel, the Northern Kingdom, and carry of its leaders into permanent exile.

587 Babylon ends the kingdom of Judah and destroys the Temple, on the 9th of Ab in the Jewish calendar.

540 Persia conquers Babylon.

538 Persia allows exiles from Judah to return to the land of Israel. The Temple is rebuilt some years later.

336–312 Alexander ends Persian rule, and bequeaths Syria-Palestine to the Seleucids, the Hellenistic Greek rulers in Antioch.

167 the revolt of the Maccabees against Antiochus Epiphanes

63 BCE Pompey conquers the Jewish state.

ca. 4 BCE Jesus is born.

ca. 30 CE Jesus is crucified.

51–57 CE Dates for the Pauline epistles

67 CE The First Jewish revolt

70 CE The Temple is destroyed, again on the 9th of Ab.

73 CE The last Jewish resistance is ended, at Masada. Mark and then Matthew and Luke are written at about this time; John is dated

anywhere from 90 CE to early second century.

131–135 The Second Jewish revolt, ending in disaster and expulsion of Jews from Jerusalem.

ca. 200 CE The Mishnah is published, by rabbi Judah the Prince/priest/patriarch.

313 CE Christianity is legalized under Constantine

325 The Council of Nicaea

438 The Theodosian code, separating the Church and Synagogue by law.

5th cent. The Talmuds emerge.

354–430 Augustine. *The City of God* was written 413–426.

ca. 500 Pseudo-Dionysus, the "Areopagite", a Christian neo-Platonist philosopher.

1265–1274 Aquinas's *Summa Theologiae*.

1285–1347 William of Ockham, nominalist philosopher.

1517 Martin Luther's 95 Theses; the Reformation begins.

1618–1648 The Thirty Years' War, a religious war, ending in exhaustion, and some small measure of religious freedom

1564–1642 Galileo Galilei.

1596–1650 René Descartes.

1687 Newton's *Principia Mathematica Philosophiae Naturalis*.

1781 Immanuel Kant, the first edition of *The Critique of Pure Reason*.

1789 The US constitution and the French revolution: disestablishment, separation of church and state, which effectively gave permission for Reform Judaism and Liberal Theology, and all the subsequent creativity of the nineteenth century.

1770–1831 G. W. F. Hegel.

1768–1834 F. D. E. Schleiermacher.

1813–1855 Søren Kierkegaard

1859 the first edition of Charles Darwin's *The Origin of Species*

1885 Julius Wellhausen, *Prolegomena to the History of Israel*, English translation: the Documentary Hypothesis.

1844–1900 Friedrich Nietzsche.

1906 Albert Schweitzer, *From Reimarus to Wrede*, translated as *The Quest of the Historical Jesus*, i. e., the failure of 19th-century German liberal historical scholarship about Jesus.

1865–1923 Ernst Troeltsch. Troeltsch was defeated by the problem of historical relativism.

1851–1930 Adolf Harnack, the dean of German Liberal theology in his time.

1914–1918 World War I.

1919 Karl Barth, the Commentary on Romans.

1938 Gerhard von Rad, "The Form-Critical Problem of the Hexateuch."

1939–1945 World War II.

1943 Martin Noth, *The Deuteronomistic History*.

1948 The Deutschmark is once again a hard currency, economic recovery in Germany begins, and Neoorthodox theology begins to lose popularity. It was a theology for hard times, which ended with economic recovery. (So Peter Berger.)

1949 Mircea Eliade, *Cosmos and History*. English translation, 1959.

1960 Thomas Kuhn, *The Structure of Scientific Revolutions*.

1984 Merold Westphal, *God Guilt and Death*.

1988 Alasdair MacIntyre solves Troeltsch's problem of historical relativity, in *Whose Justice? Which Rationality?*, in the concept of tradition-bound rationality, with considerable debts to Thomas Kuhn.

For Further Reading

The interested reader would do well to begin with the works by Mircea Eliade (*Cosmos and History*), Merold Westphal (*God, Guilt, and Death*), John Courtney Murray (*The Problem of God*). For an introduction to the Documentary Hypothesis itself, see Bernhard Anderson (an undergraduate textbook) or Richard Elliott Friedman (easier).

Akenson, Donald Harman, *Surpassing Wonder: The Invention of the Bible and The Talmuds*. New York: Harcourt Brace, 1999. Akenson shows how the Bible and the Talmuds were put together creatively, and how successive generations reshaped the structure to fit the needs of their own time.

Anderson, Bernhard, *Understanding the Old Testament*. New York: Prentice Hall, 5 edition, 2006. An excellent undergraduate introduction to the Old Testament and the history of Israel.

Augustine of Hippo, The City of God Against the Pagans. English translation by R. W. Dyson. Cambridge: Cambridge University Press, 1998.

Beck, Norman A., *Mature Christianity in the 21st Century; the recognition and repudiation of the anti-Jewish polemic in the New Testament*. New York: Crossroad, 1994. Norman Beck tracked down the mistranslations in Romans 11:28.

Bellah, Robert, "Religious Evolution." *American Sociological Review* 29 (1964) 358–374. It was reprinted in the second and third editions of William A. Lessa and Evon Z. Vogt eds., *Reader in Comparative Religion*, but not the fourth edition. It has comments on the importance of writing and iron.

Berger, Peter, *A Rumor of Angels: Modern Society and the Rediscovery of the Supernatural*. New York: Doubleday, 1969; second edition, 1990.

Berger, Peter, *The Sacred Canopy*. New York: Doubleday, 1967.

Berger, Peter, and Thomas Luckmann, *The Social Construction of Reality*. New York: Doubleday, 1966.

Blair, Alexander, *Christian Ambivalence Toward the Old Testament; Two Millennia of Neo-Platonism*. Manuscript in progress.

Boyarin, Daniel, *Border Lines: The Partition of Judaeo-Christianity*. Philadelphia: University of Pennsylvania Press, 2004.

Brague, Rémi, *Eccentric Culture: a theory of Western civilization*. Translated by Samuel Lester. South Bend, IN: St. Augustine's Press, 2002.

Brueggemann, Walter, and Hans Walter Wolff, *The Vitality of Old Testament Traditions*. Atlanta: John Knox Press, 1975. This has one very good chapter on each of J, E, D, and P.

Burleigh, Michael, *Death and Deliverance: 'Euthanasia' in Germany 1900–1945*. Cambridge: Cambridge University Press, 1994.

Burtt, E. A., *The Metaphysical Foundations of Modern Physical Science*. London: Routledge and Kegan Paul, 1924.

Cardenal, Ernesto, *The Gospel in Solentiname*, several volumes. Translated by Donald D. Walsh. Maryknoll, N.Y.: Orbis Books, 1976-1982. Rural Nicaraguans' meditations on the gospel readings, without help from scholars.

Collingwood, R. G. *An Essay on Metaphysics*. Oxford: Oxford University Press, 1940. Revised, 1998.

Depew, David J., and Weber, Bruce H., *Darwinism Evolving: Systems Dynamics and the Genealogy of Natural Selection*. Cambridge: MIT Press, 1996.

Dungan, David Laird, *History of the Synoptic Problem; The Canon, the Text, the Composition, and the Interpretation of the Gospels*. New York: Doubleday Anchor, 1999.

Dupré, Louis, *Passage to Modernity: An Essay in the Hermeneutics of Nature and Culture*. New Haven: Yale University Press, 1993. Tells how the medieval synthesis of God, man, and the world broke up on the way to the modern world.

Eliade, Mircea, *The Myth of the Eternal Return; or, Cosmos and History*. Princeton: Princeton University Press, 1954. This book was the breakthrough with respect to the differences between nature religions and historical religions.

Falk, Harvey, *Jesus the Pharisee; A new look at the Jewishness of Jesus*. New York: Paulist Press, 1985.

Friedman, Richard Elliott, *Who Wrote the Bible?* New York: Harper and Row, 1989. An excellent introduction to the Documentary Hypothesis for undergraduates and general readers.

Gallagher, Hugh Gregory, *By Trust Betrayed: Patients, Physicians, and the Licence to Kill in the Third Reich*. New York: Henry Holt, 1990. Revised edition, Arlington, VA: Vandamere Press, 1995.

Hauerwas, Stanley, *Vision and Virtue*. Notre Dame: Fides/Claretian, 1974. Contains the essay, "Love is not all you need."

Hertz, Joseph, ed., *The Authorized Daily Prayer Book* (The Siddur). New York: Bloch Pub. Co., 1974.

Heym, Stefan, *The King David Report*. Hodder and Stoughton, 1973. London: Sphere Books, 1984.

Hobbs, Edward C., "Gospel Miracle Story and Modern Miracle Stories," in *Gospel Studies in Honor of Sherman Elbridge Johnson*, ed. Massey H. Shepherd Jr. and Edward C. Hobbs. Anglican Theological Review Supplemental Series, Number Three, March 1974, pp. 117–126. http:// www.pcts.org/ journal/ miracle.html, .pdf, .dvi. This is the source for the claim that the Gospel miracle stories make sense when read in the same genre as television advertisements.

Hobbs, Edward C., "Pluralism in the Biblical Context." Discussed by the Pacific Coast Theological Society, November 16–17 1973. Reprinted in Wilhelm Wuellner and Marvin Brown, eds., *Hermeneutics and Pluralism*, Berkeley, Center for Hermeneutical Studies, 1983. It is available on-line at http:// www.pcts.org/ pluralism.html. Pluralism goes back to the earliest stages of biblical religion.

Kierkegaard, Søren, *Concluding Unscientific Postscript*. English translation by Howard V. Hong and Edna H. Hong. Princeton: Princeton University Press, 1992. See also Merold Westphal's commentary on the *Postscript*.

Kierkegaard, Søren, *The Sickness Unto Death*. English translation by Howard V. Hong and Edna H. Hong. Princeton: Princeton University Press, 1990.

Kline, Meredith G., "The Old Testament Origins of the Gospel Genre." *Westminster Theological Journal* 38 (1975) 1–27. The only published source I am aware of pointing out the parallels at the *structural* level between the Gospels and the Exodus. Edward Hobbs's work goes into great detail, but the detailed work is not yet published.

Koyré, Alexandre, *From the Closed World to the Infinite Universe.* New York: Harper and Row, 1957.

Laird, R. F. *The Boomer Bible: A Testament for Our Times.* New York: Workman Pub., 1991. The prayers are in the end of the book.

Lewis, C. S. *The Discarded Image: An Introduction to Medieval and Renaissance Literature.* Cambridge: Cambridge University Press, 1964. The world of the sixteenth century and before, lost to later imagination. Easy and fascinating.

MacIntyre, Alasdair, *Whose Justice? Which Rationality?* Notre Dame: University of Notre Dame Press, 1988.

Martin, Luther, *Hellenistic Religions: An Introduction.* New York: Oxford University Press, 1987. Informalism, the mystery religions, and Gnosticisms in the Greco-Roman world.

McCarter, P. Kyle, Jr., *Ancient Inscriptions; Voices from the Biblical World.* Washington, DC: Biblical Archaeology Society, 1996.

Murray, John Courtney, SJ, *The Problem of God.* New Haven: Yale University Press, 1964. This tells the story of the Hebrews in the desert, anxious that they were abandoned by God, just as we are anxious today.

Myers, Doris T., *C. S. Lewis in Context.* Kent, Ohio: Kent State University Press, 1994.

Neusner, Jacob, *Death and Birth of Judaism; the Impact of Christianity, Secularism, and the Holocaust on Jewish Faith.* New York: Basic Books, 1987. Reform Judaism is the first and oldest of modern Judaisms; Orthodox Judaism was a reaction to it, not merely a continuation of the pre-modern Judaism of the ghetto. Conservative Judaism came last, a mediating position between Reform and Orthodox Judaism. Christianity follows the same model: Liberal theology came before Fundamentalism, and the positions in the middle came last.

Niebuhr, H. Richard, *Radical Monotheism and Western Culture; With Supplementary Essays*. New York: Harper and Row, 1970. The essay in the end, "Faith in Gods and in God," contains on p. 122 Niebuhr's succinct statement of one central commitment of radical monotheism: that even in the disappointments of life, all of them, without exception, without reservation, ultimate reality brings good for human life.

Niebuhr, H. Richard, *The Kingdom of God in America.* New York: Harper and Row, 1937. Reprinted by Wesleyan University Press, 1988.

Niebuhr, H. Richard, *The Meaning of Revelation.* New York: Macmillan, 1940 (hardback); 1960 (paperback); Louisville: Westminster John Knox Press, 2006. The quotation about revelation and the history that makes sense of history is on p. 93 of the first edition, p. 68 of the second, and p. 50 of the third: Revelation is "that part of our inner history which illuminates the rest of it and which is itself intelligible."

Niebuhr, H. Richard, *The Responsible Self*. New York: Harper and Row, 1963.

Nof, Doron, and Nathan Paldor, "Are There Oceanographic Explanations for the Israelites' Crossing of the Red Sea?" *Bull.*

Amer. Meteorological Soc. 73 No. 3 (1992/March) 305–314. The shallow-water hydrodynamics of the parting of the Sea of Reeds in Exodus 14.

Noth, Martin, *The Deuteronomistic History*. Sheffield, UK: JSOT Press, 2001; 2nd ed. The German original was published in 1943. This is the discovery that the books of Joshua through Second Kings (excepting Ruth) came from a source the same as or close to the Deuteronomist, who put together most of what is in Deuteronomy.

Pattison, George, *A Short Course in the Philosophy of Religion*. London: SCM Press, 2001.

Pieper, Josef, *On Hope*. San Francisco: Ignatius Press, 1986.

Placher, William C., *The Domestication of Transcendence; How Modern Thinking About God Went Wrong*. Louisville: Westminster John Knox Press, 1996.

Porter, Andrew P., *Elementary Monotheism*. Lanham, MD: University Press of America, 2001. Dusty, slow, and dry.

Porter, Andrew P., "The Barbour-Smith-Gilkey Paradox: Historical Relativity in Natural Science and Historical Religion." *Theology and Science* 4 no. 1 (2006/April) 87–99. We deal with change in scientific theories easily and comfortably, so why do we have so much trouble with change in theology and history of religion?

Porter, Andrew P., *By the Waters of Naturalism: Theology Perplexed Among the Sciences*. Eugene, Oregon: Wipf and Stock, 2001.

Porter, Andrew P., *Unwelcome Good News; Providence in Human Life*. Eugene, Oregon: Wipf and Stock, 2004.

Porter, Andrew P., *Where, Now, O Biologists, Is Your Theory? Intelligent Design as Naturalism By Other Means*. Eugene, Oregon: Wipf and Stock, 2006 This contains the original exposition of volokinesis, will-directed motion.

Rowley, H. H., *The Growth of the Old Testament*. New York: Harper Torchbooks, 1963 (originally 1950). Contains a succinct summary of the evidence for the Documentary Hypothesis.

Rubenstein, Richard, *After Auschwitz; History, Theology, and Contemporary Judaism*, second edition. Baltimore: Johns Hopkins University Press, 1992. See "Modernization and the Politics of Extermination" for the elimination of undesirables in the English speaking world, and "Covenant, Holocaust, and Intifada" for the failures leading to the Holocaust.

Rummel, R. J., *Death By Government*. New Brunswick, NJ: Transaction Publishers, 1994 and 1997.

Stendahl, Krister, *Paul Among Jews and Gentiles*. Philadelphia: Fortress Press, 1976.

Von Rad, Gerhard, "The Form Critical Problem of the Hexateuch" (1938). Reprinted and translated in *The Problem of the Hexateuch and Other Essays*. London: SCM, 1966.

Welch, Claude, *Protestant Thought in the Nineteenth Century*. Two volumes. New Haven: Yale University Press, 1972 and 1985. This may seem technical and dry, but when you realize the scope of the history that has to be covered, the economy of the story and careful guidance through the thickets of a very complex century are remarkable.

Welch, Claude, "The Making of an American Mind?" Pacific Coast Theological Society, 1975; http:// www.pcts.org/ welch-hrn.html. This is background for H. Richard Niebuhr.

Westphal, Merold, *Becoming a Self; A reading of Kierkegaard's Concluding Unscientific Postscript*. Lafayette, IN: Purdue University Press, 1996.

Westphal, Merold, *God, Guilt, and Death*. Bloomington: Indiana University Press, 1984. This is a way to do philosophy of religion without cheap shots or cheap grace, but a simple typology of different basic kinds of religion. The reader in a hurry can easily begin with the last three chapters, 9–11, skipping 1–8.

White, J. Benton, *From Adam to Armageddon; A Survey of the Bible*. Belmont, CA: Wadsworth, 1994. An excellent undergraduate introduction to the whole Bible.

Yosef Hayim Yerushalmi, *Zakhor: Jewish History and Jewish Memory*. Seattle: University of Washington Press, 1996. It was first published in 1989.

Index